D1462006

Joint Ventures
for Architects
and Engineers

Joint Ventures for Architects and Engineers

DAVID R. DIBNER, AIA

McGRAW-HILL BOOK COMPANY

New York   St. Louis   San Francisco   Düsseldorf   Johannesburg
Kuala Lumpur   London   Mexico   Montreal   New Delhi
Panama   Rio de Janeiro   Singapore
Sydney   Toronto

Library of Congress Cataloging in Publication Data

Dibner, David R
Joint ventures for architects and engineers.
   1. Architectural practice. 2. Joint adventures (joint ventures) —
U.S. 3. Engineering — U.S. 4. Contractors' opera-
tions. I. Title.
NA1996.D5 658.1'144 73-39902
ISBN   0-07-016760-5

1234567890 MAMM 765432

The editors for this book were William G. Salo, Jr., and
Carolyn Nagy, the designer was Naomi Auerbach, and its
production was supervised by George E. Oechsner. It was
set in Alphatype Astro by University Graphics, Inc.

It was printed and bound by The Maple Press Company.

Photographic Credits:
Cover: The James Forrestal Building: Gil Amiaga
Pages 47 and 57: Louis Checkman
Pages 49 and 59: Gil Amiaga

to Dorothy
Mark
and Amy

Contents

Preface

"'Joint venture,' that's a dirty word." It was this phrase, over-heard by chance at a Washington, D.C., architects' gathering, that set me on a course which resulted in the writing of this book. My own experience had consistently been that this type of association could work well. As I inquired among practi-tioners in the design professions, I found out that there was much resistance toward this method of operation — mostly, I felt, through a lack of understanding of the interrelationships which must be developed to achieve success. Therefore, this book is aimed at my fellow professionals who have never tried joint venturing or who have had little or no success in its practice.

Because the principles involved in this type of relationship are simple and basic, so have I tried to keep the book. There are no startling revelations contained herein, but rather the explanation of a basic formula for interprofessional behavior, which has worked well for our firm and, when understood and correctly applied, can achieve success for others. Further, as an active architect, I have written this book from a practitioner's point of view, using lay terms and emphasizing the aspects most important to architects and engineers in their practice.

In the writing of this book, I have many people to thank. First, my wife, Dorothy, and children, Mark and Amy, who were my inspiration and whose company I missed many evenings and weekends. Then, my good friend Norman Coplan for his excellent suggestions. And, of course, my seven partners who encouraged me in this endeavor. And finally, the series of secretaries, Trish Stewart, Marion Rogers, Arlene Bury, Carol Dronke, and Dona Masini, who all did such a fine job.

David R. Dibner

Introduction

The needs of our world keep changing.

To keep pace, architects, engineers, and other design professionals charged with the responsibility of creating our physical environment may have to alter their practices in order to remain responsive. This book is intended to describe some ways in which firms can organize to meet these new challenges.

The dominant trend in today's practice of architecture and engineering is toward larger and more complex projects. All signs indicate that this trend will not only continue but most likely accelerate. As a result, the design professions have had to respond by providing a greater measure of effort in a broader range of comprehensive services. Many firms have achieved their goals by becoming larger through internal expansion or through merger.

Another method which has evolved to meet the requirements of larger and more complex projects is the formation of temporary partnerships among firms. This is called a *joint venture*.

It is the purpose of this book to describe the relationships involved in this type of organization and to provide the matrix for their development. To be successful, joint ventures must be clearly conceived and logically developed in accordance with certain basic principles. A true partnership of firms must result through a mutuality of understanding.

The formation of joint ventures has many advantages over more permanent arrangements, and it applies with equal validity to small as well as large firms. The types of associations possible are virtually unlimited, as varied as the many different kinds of projects requiring design professionals. It is the specific requirements of the project which shape the form of the joint venture. They can include not only temporary combinations among several architectural or engineering firms, but also architects with engineers, or engineers of different disciplines with each other, or any combination of the foregoing with site planners, systems developers, contractors, estimators, construction managers, soils consultants, and many others. With the increasing requirements for interdisciplinary solution of complex problems, response by joint ventures will continue to grow.

Just a word about the phrase "joint venture" which is used throughout this book. This expression has found wide acceptance by most government agencies and professional organizations in describing the temporary association of several firms. However, there appears to be concern among some practitioners. In a comment about an article by the author on joint ventures which appeared in the *AIA Journal,* there was objection voiced to the use of this term. In a letter to the editor, a Washington, D.C., architect stated his opinion that the words "joint venture" implied "commercial enterprise," which, he felt, tended to erode concepts of professionalism. Further, he stated that the term "venture" had the connotations of ". . . risk, hazard, danger, etc., whereas good professional services are directed at eliminating risks to the success of the construction undertaking, be it from the standpoint of economy, safety, function, or esthetics."

Having had wide experience with the practice of joint ventures, we cannot agree with the connotations of the words which he describes. We do, however, feel most confident that through the organization of a joint venture firms can provide the best possible professional services in the client's interest.

One further comment on the terms chosen for this book. We have taken the liberty of using "associates," "parties," "participants," and "partners" interchangeably to describe "joint venturers." These terms were used purely in an effort to create a variety of language throughout the text, without regard to the possible nuances of legal interpretation to which these words might be subject. It is our hope that the reader will look beyond any narrow meaning of these words to the broader view of the subject and to the realization that it is not words, but rather human relationships which determine the success of any venture.

Joint Ventures
for Architects
and Engineers

CHAPTER ONE

Why Joint Venture?

During the night a severe storm passes through. You awaken to find a huge tree has fallen across your driveway. Despite the efforts of your two sons and yourself, the tree won't budge. You need help. You call your neighbor who has a power-driven saw and arrange for him to cut up the tree. You and your sons will drag away the pieces and stack them in both yards. You agree to divide the firewood equally. The job gets done.

This rather simple story illustrates clearly the basic aspects of a joint venture. First, a goal which is beyond the reasonable effort of one man (firm). Next, the joining together of several men (firms) with the assignment of individual responsibilities within the common effort. Last, the carrying out of the assigned tasks.

There are many other aspects involved in joint venturing which will be discussed throughout this book. However, a very basic premise must be present to make this topic relevant to the practice of your firm. There must be a desire for change, a desire to reach beyond your present capabilities toward new goals.

In essence, this book deals with change. A planned, orderly change to the size and scope of practice in the design professions.

Is change necessary? The answer must be affirmative, no matter what the present condition and circumstance of your firm. For if you are now successful, operating at a satisfactory size and scope with an adequate return, you must change, just to remain where you are. The world around you is in a state of accelerating change. Daily, new knowledge is developed in science and technology. In addition, new and varying social and economic pressures bring change with broadest effect due to our more closely communicating world.

The relentless, positive force of change requires a response.

There is great variety in the ultimate goals of professional design firms. Obviously, the unsuccessful firm desires to be successful. Many small firms want to grow larger. Others find it necessary to grow larger to cope with larger and more complex physical design problems. The architectural firm wants to provide a greater scope of services by adding engineering capabilities. A firm wants to broaden its practice mix or enter areas peripheral to its present scope. A design firm wants to add construction capabilities. A building firm wants to provide its clients with design services. In fact, with the many different types of services required to solve today's building demands, there is virtually an unlimited variety of goals possible for firms to plan for and achieve. And of all the professions, design firms, offering skills in planning for others, should be in a position to plan the future for themselves.

ANALYZING YOUR PRACTICE

In the determination of your future, you must analyze your present practice. There are many questions which management must ask itself and answer honestly in order to plan its future. A critical self-appraisal is an important first step toward your goal. Here are three questions you might ask: Are you content with your present practice mix? Do you want to expand your scope of services? Are you satisfied with your profit picture?

1. *Are You Content with Your Present Practice Mix?*

A circumstance of success is specialization. Once you've created a bridge, or designed a house, or planned a shopping center which is recognized as being better or cheaper or outstanding in any way, chances are that you will keep on doing bridges or houses or shopping centers. In this way you continue to receive commissions in the particular field and become an "expert." Thus exclusivity and specialization set in. While at first remunerative, this process can become limiting and in some instances downright dangerous. The "hospital expert" finds it hard to get a commission for a school or church. It is even worse for the expert in carriage-house design or Romanesque architecture or the covered-wooden-bridge creator. Progress has passed them by. The broad category defined by the question of your satisfaction with your present scope of practice includes an understanding of whether you want to work in other fields, other project types, larger work, new locations, etc. Again, within the multi-faceted field of the design professions, the varieties possible are endless. It is up to you to define your goals. If they include commissions not now available to you, a joint venture may be the means of securing this work.

2. *Do You Want to Expand Your Scope of Services?*

The team approach is becoming increasingly prevalent. Providing broader, more comprehensive services as a requirement to secure and fulfill the commission is demanded by more and more clients. Your use of other firms as hired consultants in order to provide these broader skills often has certain disadvantages compared to having these complementary disciplines "in house" or more closely associated. Control of coordination and liability becomes less positive with hired consultants, and further, the project's profit becomes spread thinner, and sometimes unfairly, among all the firms.

It is the desire to provide the client with the best possible service in his interest that has led to the formation of many associations between firms of different skills. The tremendous problems posed, for instance, by the need to rebuild our cities has brought together combinations of financiers, real estate consultants, architects, engineers, sociologists, planners, systems specialists, builders, and people of many other disciplines. It must be realized that most of these additional services are presently being furnished on most of your projects by other firms. Just think about the all-encompassing breadth of the word "environment" and the scope of complementary skills necessary to achieve change in man's environment. The question then is, do *you* want to get into the act?

3. *Are You Satisfied with Your Profit Picture?*
Very few people are. However, are you doing as well as your competitors? It has generally been acknowledged that larger projects produce larger fees and larger potential for profits. The question then becomes: Are you operating on a scale broad enough to accept the bigger commissions and to take advantage of the efficiencies of a larger practice? The joint venture enables you to utilize common services in order to reduce overhead and increase net profit.

While size is no sure avenue to better profits, participating in a joint venture and temporarily "trying on" a new size through combination with others can provide the framework for better understanding of your own practice. You will see as this theme is developed later in this book that this type of "trial marriage" enables you to measure your firm's capabilities in many aspects of administration and operation.

An essential factor in practicing as a member of a joint venture is that you can secure work which is beyond your present capacity to obtain and produce, before any permanent changes in your firm are necessary. Your part of the effort is measured by your ability.

In any analysis of your firm's capability and potential it must be repeated that some change is always necessary just to keep in the same place. However, if you want to step out into a larger size or a broader scope of practice, a determined, planned effort must be made.

ACHIEVING CHANGE

If you have reviewed your practice and set new goals for a larger or different type of practice, the next step is to map ways of achievement. Three ways are available for the accomplishment of your growth aims: internal change, merger with other firms, and the formation of joint ventures.

Internal Change

The system of internal change is the most usual method for a firm to increase in size or scope. By hiring additional personnel of the same or complementary skills, the firm's staff enlarges and its capability increases. In addition, by restructuring the organization to provide a broader distribution of decision making and responsibilities, expansion is achieved at the top, assuring that management and professional skills will be adequate for the growth in size.

There are, however, a number of aspects which must be considered before starting on this path toward change.

The significant question is: Do you really want a larger firm?

Especially in the design professions, size seems to have an inverse relationship to the personal gratification or "spiritual remuneration" one receives from his work. The pattern is that the larger the firm, the further the principal retreats from personal involvement in the design and production aspects while he takes on the administrative burdens. He directs others in doing a job that, in most cases, he used to do better himself.

Who will assume the greater obligations of a larger firm? Internal growth means a more permanent type of change. Can you make the necessary modifications in management, personnel policies, facilities, and financing to accommodate this internal change? The financial aspects of the larger firm, especially partnerships, can become overwhelming. It requires new lines of credit and larger reserves to meet the cash flow of larger payrolls, accounts payable and receivable, and possibly, most difficult of all, a continuing increase in the volume of new commissions. If you do not want to take on these added burdens, the path of internal expansion may not be for you.

A further question is whether internal change can take place fast enough to meet your objectives. There has been an increasing shortage of skilled manpower to meet the needs of the professions. As a result, dramatic growth is rare. And so the firm size increases slowly, as does the practice. Trying to staff up suddenly to meet the manpower requirements of a much larger new project usually ends unhappily because of the need to rely on a large percentage of newer, untrained personnel with inadequate supervision.

The survival of a firm depends upon its ability to attract new business. Will internal change increase your ability to obtain work? Unfortunately, this is usually not the case. Unless you are adding top-level management personnel with contacts of their own, a slowly expanding firm must continue to rely on the business-getting abilities of the original principals. Can you continue to supply the enlarged firm with sufficient new business over the long run? That's a difficult question to answer.

In summary, change through internal expansion of your present firm is the most natural and usual; if controlled carefully, it represents a most desirable way to achieve change. Unfortunately, however, internal expansion is not a solution for the requirement of quick growth or increased business development capability. In addition, it is a permanent, inflexible method of change.

Merger as a Method for Growth

Another avenue for growth is through merger with other firms. It has been said that "the urge to merge is as old as Adam and Eve." And well it may be, since this method has recently found great favor throughout the field of business and has led to the formation of great corporate entities and conglomerates. These combinations may take many different forms, from the very large corporation swallowing up a small firm to the joining of two or more small companies.

Similarly in the design professions the forms of merger vary greatly. The combinations may be between firms either of different disciplines, such as architects joining with engineers, or engineers of varied specialties, such as a structural engineer joining with a mechanical/electrical engineering firm. Some mergers closely resemble those in big business in which a large financial institution will absorb a professional design firm. Examples are the merger of the Ogden Corporation with Charles Luckman, Inc., architects; the

Bangor Punta Corporation, a holding company or "conglomerate," and Metcalf and Eddy, Inc., engineers. More recently, design professionals have gone outside of the professional area to join with construction firms to give them a design-build capability. For instance, Gibbs and Hill, Inc., a long-established engineering firm, joined with Dravo Corporation to add a construction capability and thereby render their competitive position more favorable.

For the design professions, however, the merging of two or more firms can cause a number of potential problems, which should be carefully examined before contemplating merger.

Most state licensing laws still place design firms in special categories, with the principal having a personal obligation and liability for the performance of the firm. Further, both governmental and professional authorities look with careful scrutiny at the merger of a professional and a nonprofessional firm, such as engineers with contractors. They question whether the resultant design firm will be subject to undue influence from the nonprofessional which might affect the unbiased, disinterested judgment, the hallmark of the design professional.

In addition to professional considerations, the proprietors of firms contemplating merger must ask themselves what will be the effect of the union on their control of the combined entity. How will it affect their status? Their identity? In many instances the principal trades control of his firm for a more secure future.

The resultant change felt in some degree by both parties is the change of identity. The principal partner of John Jones, Engineers, a subsidiary of Peter Smith, Inc., is a different John Jones. And what of the identity and welfare of Jones' senior employees? This type of change can be very threatening to their security. Further, care must be taken to assure that John Jones be allowed to continue to act in an unfettered manner with the unbiased attitude required of him by law and the ethics of his profession.

Indeed, the merger route is a quick, dramatic way of increasing the size or scope of a firm. Through a simple signing, a firm becomes capable of obtaining and producing a contract which was formerly too large or otherwise beyond its capability. The degree of change for the firms involved in a merger will vary greatly. One thing is certain, however; merger involves a permanent restructuring and is not to be entered into without very careful consideration and professional help.

Joint Venture as a Vehicle for Change

The third path to achieve the goals of change and broader capability is through the formation of *joint ventures*. This direction seems to offer most of the advantages of the other methods of internal change and merger while limiting the disadvantages.

First let us define a joint venture. It is the *temporary* contractual association of independent firms to obtain a particular project and/or to perform a range of services. The word "temporary" is stressed because unlike the other two methods of change, a joint venture is a partnership with a limited purpose, namely, to execute a specific commission. This temporariness allows participating parties to return to their original status at the conclusion of the venture's operation, often richer and certainly wiser. There are many other important advantages of this type of practice which are worth careful consideration.

This method does not require any major restructuring of your present organization. The beauty is that you "come as you are." Each firm is expected to contribute what it presently has. The combination of *existing skills* is the strength of this type of operation. In addition this type of association provides a great deal of flexibility. In essence, you pick your partner to provide the skills you lack so that together you are able to respond to the requirements of the particular project. The possible "partnerships" include one or more firms of skills the same as or complementary to your own, large or small firms, in locations near or distant. This flexibility of combination is an important advantage in obtaining the project because it permits a team of the strongest, widest skills to be amassed.

For example, the Atomic Energy Commission decided to build a 200-billion-electron-volt atom smasher at a construction cost estimated at $250 million. The design of this unique project required a combination of expertise in architecture, engineering, and construction. There was no one company available to perform all the work required by this large and complex installation. Finally selected was DUSAF, a joint venture composed of: Daniel, Mann, Johnson, and Mendenhall, architects and engineers of Los Angeles, California; the office of Max O. Urbahn, architects of New York; Seelye, Stevenson, Value, and Knecht, Inc., consulting engineers of New York; and the George A. Fuller Company, building constructors of Dallas, Texas. While some members of this group had worked together before, all four joined for the first time for the specific purpose of designing and constructing this largest research plant ever built.

In its basic elements this example is typical of the reason for and value of joint ventures: a specific program requiring that a group of firms be formed for the purpose of responding to a specific set of requirements, each firm with specific tasks to perform within the framework of the total project.

Another distinct advantage of the joint venture method is that it enables a firm either to try out the larger work or to enter new fields without making a permanent commitment to the future and risking capital beyond its means. Especially in this world of complex and concentrated projects is this advantage genuine. A firm is able to respond to change by creating a new combination of capabilities fashioned to the needs of the particular complex. As a result, the joint venture participation provides the background and experience in fields which normally are foreign to the practice of a particular firm. An architectural firm, for example, may be exposed to engineering projects through participation with an engineering firm in a joint project, and unlike the case where they employ engineering consultants, the architectural firm can share liabilities in fields of limited expertise. An unlimited number of new avenues of experience are possible in size and scope of project when you consider all the combinations possible involving the many different types of firms now involved in the environmental design field.

Another important positive aspect of a joint venture is that the identity of the individual firm is rarely lost. Firm A joins Firm B, and Firm A and B results rather than a new Firm C.

This retention of individual identity negates one of the disadvantages of the merger in which identity is lost. Further, based upon the understandings developed at the outset of the project, it is possible, if desired, for each of the firms to be identified with all aspects of the project regardless of the individual responsibilities of each firm and thus to take individual credit for the entire operation. In other instances, where the parties so agreed, the credit for each firm would be clearly related to its responsibilities within the venture. Again, the enormous flexibility available in this type of organization.

An advantage to your client of joint venturing should not be overlooked. By reviewing the roster of joint venture partners, the client is assured that a full complement of talents is available for his project. This depth of manpower or breadth of capability potential offered by the combination of firms becomes an important factor to the client in his selection procedures. In many instances the right *team*, able to demonstrate proper organization, has been selected over the single firm because of demonstrably broader combined capacity, background, and experience.

Speed of staffing in joint ventures is greater than in the internal-growth method. Remember, in forming the joint venture, you are marrying (on a temporary basis) two or more functioning firms complete with manpower and management. Normally, little employee recruiting is required to staff the project. The leadership is ready as well. This aspect can be most important to the client who requires a quick start and a compressed project schedule. Another factor contributing to a faster project takeoff results from the combination of proper backgrounds in the joint venture members; thus, you have combined the proper skills, ready for action. No time is lost in learning the basic criteria necessary for the particular project.

An example of this type of operation was our experience in the case of an airline which wanted to build a reservation center in New Jersey on an extremely tight time schedule. The joint venture created to meet the client's specific needs was the selection of a North Carolina architect, who furnished direct knowledge on the design of this type of installation, having done several before, and our firm, which provided the local know-how, manpower, and management skills. Each firm did what it knew best without the necessity of pausing for new learning, and so the client received a building responsive to his design and time requirements.

But the client alone did not benefit. Each firm in that joint venture learned something from the other. This aspect illustrates another advantage of this type of operation. It enables each of the participants to learn how the other operates and to benefit through the application of these newly learned skills to his own practice. Remember, in this case, you are not learning theory but rather applied procedures which have been developed, practiced, and proved by a successful firm. This exchange of information is equally valid if the combination involves firms of different disciplines or if it includes the joining of several firms in the same field. Especially administrative and office procedures benefit from this learning process. One cannot overemphasize the value that this aspect can have to the individual firm or the effect on its future profit picture.

Joint venturing is a method of producing very large projects without straining the full capacity of your office. Flexibility of action is severely curtailed when one project occupies the total productivity of your firm. Repetitive and valuable clients may be lost as a result of your inability to respond to their needs because you are overloaded with other work. Joint ventures allow you to spread the load and utilize your manpower most effectively. At the time of this writing our firm is engaged in eight joint venture operations whose total scope is more than four times the total productive capacity of the firm. Yet because the load is balanced between all efforts, and the timing of the projects is carefully scheduled, we are able to devote approximately three-fourths of our manpower to the production of our own work to the satisfaction of our own clients.

The new experiences gained in joint venturing create a broader background for your firm which in turn provides the vehicle for obtaining further work. If, for example, a firm is interested in entering the field of hospital design but has no experience at all in this type of facility, one of the potential avenues is to joint venture with a firm qualified in hospital design. Why should the other firm be interested in joining with you? Because you may offer, through the uniqueness of your practice, something of value to the other firm, e.g., management, manpower, a definite client, proximity to site, etc. For it is only where there is a mutual exchange of value that a joint venture can be successful.

For example, a post-office project is proposed for a certain community, and local architects are being interviewed. Among the criteria the Post Office Department uses in the selection is its desire to employ a local architect, the firm's manpower and capability to perform the work, and experience in the design of postal facilities. A local firm too small for this project size and without post-office experience contacts a firm in another city who had the necessary manpower and who had previously designed several postal facilities. They join together, each pooling his particular capability, in order to secure and produce the project. This leads to the last and possibly the greatest advantage: the increased ability to secure the commission. The combination of several firms' talents also means the pooling of contacts, promotional materials, and job development know-how. All of this tends to assure that the venture has the best possible chance of getting the job.

With all these advantages, why is this form of joint practice not more prevalent? Especially in this world of ever-broadening challenges which requires a team of many different types of expertise combined to respond to the specific challenge, cooperation between firms becomes vital. The lack of broader acceptance of this type of association is most likely a result of an absence of real understanding of the basic contributing factors necessary for a successful relationship. As a result there may have been many experiences which proved less than successful for the participants.

Certainly, where relationships between human beings are involved, there is no sure formula guaranteeing success. Just look at the divorce statistics as a demonstration of this fact. However, where intelligent understanding forms the basis of the union, chances are that the results will well reward the efforts.

This book will deal with methods of assuring this cooperative effort.

CHAPTER TWO

Selecting the Project

Once you have determined that the formation of a joint venture is a possible path of action for your firm, there then remains the selection of a suitable project. No matter how many experiences you may have had in this type of association, the same analytical process must be made for each new project. The importance of evaluating every project must be stressed because there are constantly changing circumstances which will influence your decision.

From the newspapers, government bulletins, conversations with others, and many diverse sources, you become aware of potential projects. In the past, if the job seemed too large for the size of your practice, it was not even considered. Now, with the possibility of the association of other firms to share the load, the potential to secure the commission becomes greater and is worth further consideration. The opportunity is yours to enter new fields and enlarge your practice—at least to "try it on for size." The required effort is minimal.

The criteria for evaluating a project for the possibilities of joint venturing are deceptively simple. Ask yourself two basic questions: (1) can your firm alone *secure* the commission, and (2) does your firm alone have the capacity to *produce* the project? If the answer is "no" to either question, then there exists the possibility of associating with others in a joint venture in order to provide a positive response to the question. As described in the first chapter, there are other methods of response such as merger and internal change; however, their applications are limited by their negative qualities. Further, because these methods involve permanent organizational changes, they are very rarely employed to meet the demands of one particular project.

Another response could be through the use of hired consultants. However, this approach may not place your firm in the best competitive position. The client is often looking for a combination of disciplines, with each firm having prime responsibility in its field of expertise. Further, consultants are often not in the best position to help your firm secure the project, since the majority of their contacts are with firms like your own, rather than with owners.

The premise is that you have analyzed the situation, rejected the alternatives, and decided to try an association with other firms.

As you realize, there are many factors which deserve consideration in deciding which is the proper project to secure. In effect, you must analyze the project's requirements, review your firm's capacity to respond, and then note the differences between the two. This analysis defines the help you need from others.

GETTING THE JOB

How does the design professional secure a commission? Enough has been written about this subject to fill many books much larger than this one. However, the basic criteria seldom change. The most capable firm usually will get the job. In this instance, the definition of "most capable" must be broadened to include many divergent abilities, from the strongest and most direct client contacts all the way to the greatest technical skills. This book will describe a method to increase your ability to get the job.

Most owners with whom we have spoken are very logical in their criteria for selection. They are measuring your ability to meet their needs. While fancy frills in presentation must sway some, and politics may decide the successful selection on others, in the long run it is still capability that counts. Large corporations and governmental bodies must have substance on which to base their decisions, for usually the selectors are in a position where they must justify their choice to their superiors and in many instances to the firm's stockholders or the government's citizens.

Of interest is the fact that with the possibility of joint venturing your professional horizons now broaden. No longer are you restricted by your own limitations in the selection of potential projects. The field is as wide as your own creative ability to conceive combinations of talent. Potential projects which you could not contemplate before, because they required a size or scope larger than your capacities, now become real possibilities. The future is yours.

Let us assume that you have learned about a large project and you would like to secure the design commission. You must first decide if you have a chance to land it by yourself. Certainly if you can obtain it and produce it alone, there is no need to consider a joint venture. However, if it looks like a difficult commission, it is worth evaluating to assess the possibilities. Each project is different and carries with it varying criteria for selection. The procedure involves compiling both a list of the important considerations influencing the client's judgment in his selection process and an honest evaluation of your firm's abilities to respond. Thus, in examining some of the criteria for selection, a checklist of requirements and responses can be formulated.

What Are the Required Skills?

Careful analysis must be made of what major categories of expertise will be needed to fulfill the owner's needs. Will there be architecture, site planning, mechanical or electrical or structural engineering? Are acoustics or space planning or one of the hundred other allied fields a major consideration? Will the owner expect a financing or construction capability? Or, perhaps, will the addition of any of these capabilities strengthen the possibility of your selection?

Most often a specific project does not fall totally within the bounds of any one design discipline. Very rare is the demand for all architecture or all engineering. Usually the scope of the project contains many and varied requirements. This fact becomes most evident when one realizes the tremendous scope of environmental design which embraces the sociological and psychological aspects in addition to the physical and economic needs of human existence.

In responding to the requirements of a project, a firm usually supplies skills either from in-house capabilities or through the employment of consultants in order to provide the necessary expertise. In making his selection the owner looks for assurance of major strength in all the important fields of required talent. As a result, he may favor the firm that has the internal capabilities to fulfill all roles. Further, he may feel that better coordination of efforts results from the combination of all skills under one roof. There are many instances in which architectural firms, using consultants for engineering, have lost the commission to architecture–engineering firms who convinced the owner that this combined internal capability was in the owner's best interest.

On the other hand, the company which has to rely on outside consultants often advances a strong argument in defense of this method of operation. They state that through the careful selection of their consultants, they are able to choose the specific consulting firm most capable of performing the particular project. In addition, through the flexibility afforded by a choice of many consultants, they can assure the owner that the project will be adequately staffed by experts with background in the skills required. Furthermore, they are choosing from among firms who are competing in their respective fields and therefore must keep current in order to survive. These consultants may also possess a much broader background as a result of having served as consultants for many other firms. In comparison, the in-house staff, as "consultants" for only one firm, may tend to stagnate and service the project less efficiently because they are not motivated by the necessity to compete in their field.

The joint venture method benefits from the best of both practices. It provides the owner with the sharpened skills of the competitive firms of each field under an administrative organization which assures better coordination.

As projects become more complex and clients more demanding, the much broader response from combinations of many disciplines is especially significant. The trend is definitely moving toward the team approach of complementary skills.

Necessary Background and Knowledge

So often, in interviews for possible contracts, the question is asked, "Have you ever done a hospital (or college or library or post office, boys' camp, etc., as the case may be) before?" No client, it seems, wants to be the first to train you in a specific type of project. If you haven't designed a similar project previously, there is usually some quick footwork to do to convince the client you still have the goods.

> CLIENT: Have you ever designed a tungsten-molybdenum plant before?
>
> ARCHITECT NO. 1: No, we have not, but the problem is probably not much different from our last project, a manufacturing plant for the Apex Safety Pin Company. Let me show you how we approached that project, because your requirements seem to be very similar. [He opens the brochure.]

Or a more creative response, which sometimes works.

> ARCHITECT NO. 2: No sir, we have never had the opportunity to design a tungsten-molybdenum plant, and that is where you are in luck. We will solve your problem with an entirely new approach, unfettered by past solutions which probably no longer apply. Through our experience in shopping centers we have developed certain unique methods for handling materials and circulation which we feel could well fit your needs.

If you've ever done this type of "come-from-behind" selling, you know how tough it is. Especially are young firms in this dilemma. They have no vast portfolio of experience to draw upon. For the small firm particularly, the joint venture can help in this regard through the "instant experience" provided by a partner firm.

Necessary Contacts

Let's face reality. *What* you know is not necessarily, totally, unequivocably that which secures the commission. In many instances *who* you know is important. As a consequence, in analyzing your ability to secure the project, you must ask whether obtaining the particular job requires strong contacts. And if the answer is "Yes," whether you have the necessary contacts or whether you need help. Certainly, one way to get help is from another firm who might have better job-development potential but who lacks your firm's abilities in other areas. The combination of talents will place both firms in a better position to secure the commission.

PRODUCING THE PROJECT

One of the main factors which influences the selection of a particular project as worthwhile for joint venturing is your firm's capacity to produce the project once you've received the commission. The ability to produce and the ability to secure the project are closely related. Simply stated, if you obviously can't turn out the job, what makes you think the owner will be willing to entrust his project to you in the first place!

Some of the areas for self-examination of your firm regarding your ability in producing the work include manpower requirements, financing the project, management skills, and administrative functions.

Manpower Requirements

Knowing the approximate number of men and their duration on the project is an important parameter in the analysis of a potential project. Through experience it is usually possible to estimate the man-days required to finish a project. In fact, many government agencies in their fee-negotiation procedures require that the architect-engineer submit a breakdown of estimated effort for each phase of the work. A method which many firms use estimates the number of drawings which will be required and then multiplies by a standard man-day per drawing figure developed from previous work. Once you have estimated the amount and duration of manpower required by the project, the next step involves figuring out your ability to respond. An important thing to remember in relation to establishing your capacity to provide the necessary manpower skills for a particular project is that while producing the new job, you must continue the other projects of your practice. To place your full potential on one job without considering the other work of your office is unrealistic. In fact it is suicidal!

The time schedule of your work load is a factor to be carefully considered. Because projects must progress through various phases, it is possible that the apparent heavy work load in your present practice may accommodate still another large project because of timing. When the new project is started and enters the conceptual stage, the other work may have moved into the production stage, leaving the void to be filled by the new project. Other factors which influence timing are the size of your firm and the nature of your present work load. Larger offices have the flexibility of moving manpower from project to project as demanded. By "stealing" one man from several projects, you can staff the new work while maintaining adequate progress on the other projects. Further, as every experienced practitioner knows, not all projects move smoothly or at the same pace. Unanticipated lags are created by the owner's extended time requirements for decision making, approvals, internal changes, etc. These gaps can well be filled by another project. Perhaps a joint venture!

Manpower is a deceiving word. It includes staff skilled in the many different aspects required to produce a project. In this analysis it is necessary to break these skills down further. Each field of architecture and engineering has further classifications describing the work being done, such as for design (designers), contract documents (draftsmen), and construction administration (field men). By being specific as to the types required, you focus on the skills you possess and define the skills you lack to complete the work. These skills will be supplied by your joint venture partner. Quite often, a firm will find itself with a surplus of one skill and a shortage of another. This will be as a result of the practice mix at the specific moment in time or possibly the vagaries of the employment market. The idea is to seek help in the areas required . . . or the converse, find projects where you can contribute your excess manpower and idle skills. Again the beauty of the joint venture. In order to participate, it is not necessary to have all the skills in your own organization.

Financing the Project

Unfortunately, large projects need lots of money to finance the operations between receipt of payments. It is necessary to measure whether or not you have the financial support necessary to add a new big project to your work load.

Many firms succeed, through the years of their practice, in establishing a flexible line of credit from a lending institution. A substantial contract is part of the collateral assurance which the design professional shows to the bank. If you are not that secure financially, you may need help. If you are in good shape financially, there is the question whether you would prefer to put your money in something else. Either way, one of the alternatives to ensure an adequate supply of funds may be through the choice of a joint venture partner.

One of the extra advantages, by the way, of joint venturing is the ability to engage in a large practice with reduced financing.

Management Skills

There are just so many principals of a firm who provide leadership and guidance. These men serve at the heart of your business and in large measure are responsible for its success. In the operation of a joint venture, qualified management personnel are possibly more important since they operate, in a sense, independently of the home firms. The question in analyzing a potential joint venture project is whether you have within your firm the spare management and administrative capacity to take on a new large project.

Especially is this factor critical in the small firm. The one, two, or three principals are now overworking in their effort to develop and build up a practice. Can they be spared, or strained, to take on the additional load? Very often this is the hardest of the many items to evaluate. There is a tendency to underestimate the time necessary to manage a large project. A good way to bring this into focus is to ponder on the many meetings a principal is required to attend each week to keep up with his present work load.

In addition to the problem of finding available time, there is the psychological problem of the good manager's being reluctant to allow others to help him manage or manage for him. In particular, the practitioner with the small office falls into the trap of wanting to remain "his own boss" without interference in or review of his decision making. The partner in the larger office has already been through the ordeal of relying on the judgment of others and therefore is less threatened by this aspect of association. However, his insecurity may stem from the worry of who will take his place at the home office while he is "out" joint venturing. Management, the key to success in your practice, as well as in any collaboration, must be evaluated carefully.

Administrative Functions

A new large project requires office and accounting backup services. Bringing the new project into your office may strain the services that you now have or may require additional personnel and/or direction. It may be better to join with others and share this load. We have found, through the development of special systems, that the administrative functions of a joint venture can be held to a minimum and thereby have little effect on the home office.

AN EVALUATION FORM

To summarize, the question which must be asked about a potential job is whether your firm has the experience and capability to perform the work on an economically suitable basis, or is help needed. It is absolutely necessary that an honest and detailed appraisal be made of your capabilities in order to reach the proper conclusions.

In order to make this evaluation as simple as possible, our firm has developed a form (Figure 2-1) which takes no more than five minutes to fill out, while covering all pertinent areas of examination. Whether you use a similar form or the back of an envelope is immaterial. The important object is to examine the problem as critically as possible.

In column A are listed the broad requirements to secure and produce the project. Your ability to respond to the demands of the proposed project is entered as estimated percentages in column B. Naturally, these are guesses, but with ex-

EVALUATION OF POTENTIAL PROJECT

Proposed Project _____   Date _____

Location _____   Estimated Start _____

Estimated Cost _____   Estimated Duration _____
                                         (To construction
                                         start)

(A) REQUIREMENT	(B) ABILITY TO RESPOND	(C) HELP NEEDED
1. Required skills		
2. Background and experience in the specific field		
3. Contacts		
4. Manpower		
5. Financing		
6. Management		
7. Administration		

FIG. 2-1

perience they can be fairly accurate. The value of this form is that by filling in the appropriate spaces it develops in column C the definition of your joint venture partner, a profile of capability required to enhance your skills.

For illustration there is included an evaluation form (Figure 2-2) of an actual project. We had learned that a local hospital for whom we had done prior work was looking for an architect-engineer to design a new clinical facility of a highly specialized nature. The projected cost of the project was $6 million. While we were experienced in the design of hospitals, we had no former experience in the specific functions for which the new building would be used. The thinking which went into the filling out of the form was generally as follows:

EVALUATION OF POTENTIAL PROJECT

Proposed Project _MEDICAL BUILDING_   Date _1-15-69_

Location _NEWARK, N.J._   Estimated Start _4-1-69_

Estimated Cost _$6,000,000_   Estimated Duration _24 MOS._
(To construction
start)

(A) REQUIREMENT	(B) ABILITY TO RESPOND	(C) HELP NEEDED
1. Required skills	75%	25%
2. Background and experience in the specific field	25%	75%
3. Contacts	95%	5%
4. Manpower	50%	50%
5. Financing	100%	—
6. Management	100%	—
7. Administration	100%	—

FIG. 2-2

1. *Required Skills:* We rated ourselves 75% because we had designed quite a few hospitals and related facilities; however, we had never done this specific type of building.

2. *Background and Experience in the Specific Field:* We knew that the client wanted specific expertise in this building type. We had no actual experience in this area; however, we had designed hospitals, and so the 25% rating.

3. *Contacts:* Having done work for this client before, we were confident in this area; therefore 95%. By the way, unless the client is a close relative and has absolute power of decision, we never estimate our ability at 100%.

4. *Manpower:* We were very busy, and we had another large job of higher priority about to break. New manpower

was tough to obtain. While a new $6 million project would not put that much of a load on our staff, we could easily take half of the effort without excessive strain. In the appropriate column 50% was entered.

5. *Financing:* We had a good line of credit and were in good shape. 100%,

6. *Management:* Our partner who had handled most of our other hospital work and was familiar with this client appeared to have uncommitted time. Our Project Director, skilled in this area, was scheduled to be free at about the right time. This area looked solid. 100%.

7. *Administrative:* We were okay in this area. Probably we would have to hire another bookkeeper, but they weren't too hard to find. 100%.

The result of this quick survey is the list of complementary talents required of an associate to assist in obtaining and producing the project. The description of our potential partner emerged. We needed a firm with background in the design of this building type, which was able to take on half of the manpower load. Why would our theoretical partner need us? Mainly for our ability to supply contacts and manpower. We were also in a position to supply the financing, management, and administrative skills.

Organizing your evaluation of a possible project through the use of this simple form can be extremely helpful. In essence, it forces you to think objectively in the various categories which are the keys to the success of a project. In a few minutes' time you are able to "think out" the project and its effect on your firm. And should you decide to pursue the commission, it goes one step further; it produces the profile of your potential partner.

You are now ready to seek him out and go for the commission.

CHAPTER THREE

Choosing Your Partner

The selection of an associate with whom to joint venture is certainly not as difficult as choosing a wife. Neither is the union made in heaven nor is it as long-lasting as a marriage. Although with the divorce rate accelerating and project schedules consistently delayed, the last statement may soon no longer be true. However, since the choice of a joint venture partner can greatly influence your business life, it should be thoughtfully considered and carefully consummated.

What are you looking for? If you have gone through the analysis contained in the previous chapter, the description of your partner should be fairly clear. Your partner's firm has the skills necessary to complement your firm; the sum of the two form a capability for direct response to the requirements of the project.

It is possible that the selection of a joint venture partner is an excellent application for computer technology. All firms interested in joint venturing submit their available skills for retention in the memory bank, and upon call, the computer prints out a list of eligible associates who can meet the criteria of a specific job. If computer dating can become so popular, why not computer associating? However, in the absence of an automated means of selection, more human methods will have to be used.

TYPICAL COMBINATIONS

Since the types of joint ventures are so many and varied, the possibilities of combinations are almost infinite. Therefore, before we recount some of the ways to find potential partners, it would be best to take a moment to review some of the typical combinations which have developed through the years.

"Shotgun Marriages"

This type of combination seems to originate mostly from government agencies. In their anxiety both to assure themselves that the work will be adequately staffed and to spread the work among as many tax-paying citizens as possible, government agencies often create their own combinations of firms. The construction agency of most government departments, such as the Public Building Service of the General Services Administration (GSA) or the construction branches of the military services, have on file the brochures of many qualified professional firms. With the requirement to secure design services for a specific project, a list of the most eligible firms will be compiled. When the project is of sufficient size to warrant the selection of several firms, the agency may designate the top two or three firms on its list as associate firms and suggest that a joint venture be formed among them to develop the work. Sounds like a strange way to find a partner. Yet the designs of many of the largest buildings throughout the country have been successfully accomplished by joint ventures formed in this way.

To the credit of the government agencies involved, realizing that the success of their own projects are at stake, they usually are very careful in the selection of the firms to be combined. Where both architecture and engineering are involved to an approximately equal degree, they will frequently combine an architectural and an engineering firm. Where they would like to be assured of high quality of design along with efficient performance, they will combine a well-known design firm with a company which has built its reputation on timely and economic performance.

An example of this type of joint venture occurred in 1961, when three firms from diverse parts of the country were called to GSA in Washington, D.C. For the first time in their lives, N. C. Curtis, Jr., of New Orleans, Louisiana, William Hamby of New York, New York, and Bernard Grad of Newark, New Jersey, met each other. At that time they were told that they had been selected to design the $38 million James Forrestal Building (FOB No. 5) in Washington, D.C. From this meeting emerged the joint venture of Curtis and Davis, Fordyce and Hamby Associates, and Frank Grad & Sons, a joint venture which produced the largest government office building in the nation's capital. The building construction was completed in 1969. During these eight years the joint venture proved a truly rewarding experience for all involved and produced an outstanding building.

Unfortunately, in some instances, some government combinations result from reasons other than competence, with the result that both the design and the designers are apt to suffer. This might best be illustrated by some of the poor government works one is apt to see around the country. However, most often where the participants are chosen carefully and procedures such as those which will be outlined in this book are carefully followed, the results for all concerned can be very beneficial.

Combining Technical Competence with Geographical Proximity

Most clients would like to have the best of all worlds. A new factory is to be built in Podunk, Pennsylvania. This project represents a substantial investment for the parent company, as well as a significant step forward in the firm's development. The clients want the new building to reflect the most advanced thinking in plant design. They also feel that there is much in the development of the project which can only come from an understanding of the company and local conditions. In addition, it's good business to help out the local professionals. In many instances, hearings must be held with the local planning board, which may have heretofore shown a lack of sympathy for the "foreign" big-town firms with their high-pressure ways. The solution to it all is the combination of the big-city expertise and experience with local understanding.

Often, if the project is really remote and the local procedures different, a firm is wise to find and join with a local company. This is especially helpful during the construction stage of the work. The nearby firm loses much less time in travel and in assimilating local conditions.

At other times the client will go to one of the participants and suggest that he collaborate with the other firm. If the request is from the local plant manager, it is usually made to the small firm with a suggestion that it contact a large firm of its own choosing to supply the modern technological thinking. Just as often, the corporate headquarters in the big city contacts the larger firm and suggests the reverse procedure.

And so a different type of joint venture is born. Note that each participant brings to the union his own expertise. Note also that none of the parties is forced to combine. The freedom of commitment still rests with each firm.

We formed this type of venture when we were engaged by the Third Air Force USAFE to design NATO bases throughout France. We joined with the American engineering firm of Seelye, Stevenson, Value, and Knecht; because we knew little about construction in France, the joint venture hired a firm of French architects, André and Claude DuFau of Paris, to produce the work. The collaboration worked extremely well. A joint venture office was established in Paris, staffed by members of both firms. The management and design direction were furnished by our office, and since the drawings and specifications had to be produced in French and in the metric system, most of the production of construction documents was accomplished by local personnel.

The Combination of Job Getter and Project Producer

There are many occasions when a small firm is in a position to obtain work which is well beyond its capacity to produce. This firm might have developed a prior relationship with a client whose needs have now exceeded the professional's production capabilities. Often the response is to try to suddenly "staff up" to meet the challenge. Unfortunately this effort often meets with limited success, because it is almost impossible for management to grow at the required rate. The result: a poorly managed project with many potential problems. Many times an alternate answer is to seek a larger, experienced firm as a partner to supply the needed skills and manpower. One of the reasons why this method is not too popular is because of the reluctance of the small firm to expose its coveted client to the large firm. However, often the client-professional relationship sinks and severs because of the professional's attempt to bite off more than he can chew, with the result that no more jobs are forthcoming after the disaster.

It has been demonstrated that in the joint venture of this type, wherein each firm's responsibilities are clearly designated and the proper interrelationship is established, much can be done to prevent problems from arising.

For example, there was an occasion in which our firm participated as a "big brother" architectural firm. The smaller engineering firm brought the project to us, and we carefully defined a relationship which included the stipulation that they were to direct all presentations to the owner and participate in all meetings and discussions with the client. We remained in the background and produced almost the entire project. All this was achieved with the owner's full knowledge. The commission is finished, and the other firm has received further work from the client. They were just in again to talk about another large project they will be getting and asked whether we would like to form a new joint venture.

The Interdisciplinary Approach

This method of association is similar to the practice of a group of medical specialists. In the design professions a similar need has arisen. How can a single design discipline solve the problems of housing or highways or mass transit? Experts from many varied fields all contribute to the solution of complex problems. I am reminded of a fascinating quotation from a speech of Robert L. Durham, FAIA, former president of the American Institute of Architects:

> I happen to be an advisor to a highway team in Seattle. It is fascinating to discover how much there is to learn from each other. The sociologist member of the team recently inquired, in a new kind of cost accounting, how many divorces per mile the highway planners were willing to accept. He pointed out, sensibly enough, that destruction of housing and neighborhood affects family life and, inevitably, marital relationships. We have found no easy answer to his question. But the fact that it was asked has served to broaden our understanding a little bit more.

In this type of combination there may be a mixture of one, several, or all of the following:

Architect	Sociologist
Engineer	Psychologist
Planner	Economist
Landscape architect	Financier
Systems analyst	Computer expert
Real estate consultant	Construction contractor

There are many aspects peculiar to these types of combinations and more will be written about this in later chapters.

Reinforcement of Similar Skills

Probably the most usual joint ventures are made up of a partnership of firms of similar skills. Architects join with architects, or engineers with engineers, to meet the challenge of a large project. This assures the client that there will be enough manpower to staff all required functions.

For the New Jersey College of Medicine and Dentistry, a $150 million project, three architectural firms were united to pool their resources. Each firm contributed manpower to a separate joint venture office. The largest office, Eggers and Higgins, was made supervising architects, with Frank

Grad & Sons and Gilbert L. Seltzer named associate architects. Normally these firms, all from the same geographic location, were competitors for the same projects. However, the result of this association was a harmonious relationship that produced a well-designed complex.

The Design-Production Team

Offices vary in ability. Especially among architectural firms, certain offices become recognized for their design abilities, others for their production capabilities and attention to detail. As a result, there has developed a new type of combination of firms. Artists and artisans, so to speak. In this way the owner is assured of the best of both worlds: the design firm with its ability to turn out outstanding creations and the no-nonsense firm to assure low-cost, timely production, and errorless construction documents. This combination can work well; however, trouble may result from the owner's dictating which firms are to form the association.

This type of combination can be very successful when properly established. However, when poorly conceived, it led to one of the few joint ventures from which we emerged saddened but wiser. We were asked (rather forcefully) by a client to combine with another firm from another city. They were designated as the designers and we as the producers. A very tight budget was established and the venture went forth. The principal of the design firm was a prominent practitioner who had many young graduates on his staff. They proceeded to design a complex whose cost was in excess of the project budget. When reminded of this fact, our partners literally shrugged their shoulders and suggested that the design was their responsibility and the construction cost was in our domain. Further, because of their lack of practical experience, many aspects of the design contained details which were virtually unbuildable. Again, that was our problem. The conclusion, with a client whose construction budget was law: we ended up doing a good measure of redesign, in addition to taking on our original responsibilities for the contract documents and construction administration. From this experience we discovered that it is impossible to separate the design phase from the rest of the project; the designer must have a continuing responsibility throughout the project. We learned how important it is for the success of a joint venture that continuing communication and the sharing of responsibilities be maintained throughout the duration of the association.

The Design-Build Team

With the arrival of the "package builder" on the construction scene, there was much reexamination of position among design professionals, especially architects. How to compete against the advantages claimed by the design-construct combinations? One of the effective responses has been the joint venture combination of a design firm and a construction firm. The advantages of this combination are several. As with the package builder, the owner is dealing with one entity, a joint venture, which can provide the same efficiency and cost guarantees. An additional advantage to the owner, which the competitive system does not have, is that the design firm of the project is readily identifiable and their abilities and background clearly defined. They are not just the "design arm" of a construction company. The design firm in the joint venture continues to exert a professional influence on the project and can maintain a relationship with the client which is more direct.

The understanding which must be developed between the design and construction firms in this type of combination is different, to a degree, from that established between design professional firms. Beside the fact that usually this association deals with a greater amount of funds, there are "nonprofessional" relationships with subcontractors and material suppliers which must be made clear. Of great importance, too, is who will have the deciding role when questions related to design and extra construction cost are involved. Chapter 12, which reviews the relationships developed, will contain information about the important aspects of this type of alliance.

Other Forms of Joint Ventures

There are many other combinations possible. For instance, in addition to the designer-builder team, there is the designer-builder-landowner trio which, in turn, could be made into a quartet of designer-builder-landowner-financier.

The variety of direction which is possible within the framework of joint venture is one of its great strengths. It provides unlimited horizons for response to environmental problems. However, despite the type and complexity possible in joint ventures, equitable, efficient, and effective arrangements are possible by following the path of early agreement on certain basic matters.

SOURCES OF PARTNERS

After you have analyzed your goals, determined to joint venture, selected the project, and defined the type of partner you require, the next step is to go about finding him. It has been our experience that there are many available sources of potential partners. All it takes is positive action on your part.

At the outset, it is important to note that while there is some advantage in choosing a partner who is personally familiar to you, it is far from a necessity. In fact, it would be foolhardy to limit your range of selection to familiar firms. From the many fruitful experiences we have had in joint venturing with new faces, the need for prior acquaintance with the principals of the new firm would rate fairly low on our list of requirements.

What are you looking for? A firm with proven strength in the areas in which you lack the capabilities. A reputable firm. A solvent firm. A compatible firm. Familiarity will come as the association develops. It is a strange fact to realize, but our experience has shown that a majority of our successful ventures (and the feeling of success must be a mutual one among all venturers) was achieved with firms which were strangers to us at the commencement of the venture. The ways to find a partner firm for an association are many and varied, once you have defined your goals. Remember that at the same time you are looking, there are probably other firms looking for you!

Probably the best sources for the discovery of collaborators are your business and professional organizations. At meetings or conventions, conversations arise quite normally about various aspects of practice. It is a perfect place to gauge interest and discuss the possibilities of joint venturing. There must be a positive attitude on your part. You are offering to join the real qualities of your firm's strength with another firm. Probably the most difficult situation is to offer to join with another firm in the same field. This firm, normally your competitor through the years, is now proffered the possibility of participating as a partner. This requires a new understanding of your role. But the realization on the part of each firm that without the other there is little or no possibility of getting the commission should aid in the understanding. We have found that, with rare exception, the discussion of potential projects with other practitioners has been a rewarding experience.

Do not limit your contacts to merely your own professional organizations. Gatherings of other professionals are just as valid. Often members of the AIA attend meetings of the Consulting Engineers Council (CEC) and the National Society of Professional Engineers (NSPE) and find the information gathered there of help in the selection of associates. Business clubs such as the Lions, Elks, and Rotary are also good listening posts for what is happening. Material suppliers and even insurance salesmen can also be most helpful as sources of information.

How often have you read a professional journal or related magazines which have described a successful project? These articles serve to introduce you to the skills of other firms and possible partners. For example, there was our decision to seek the commission for an extensive development of an island site. Our analysis indicated that we lacked strength in the design of docks and port facilities. A professional magazine contained an article about a unique solution to a difficult port problem by an engineering firm who specialized in this area. Contact was made, discussions were held, and we decided to join forces to seek the commission.

Often it is the client who dictates or suggests a partner. Where you are commanded to choose a specific firm, there is usually no choice except to accept or reject the client's instruction. This should be done after meeting with the other firm and objectively discussing the partnership possibilities.

Enough time should be allowed to get to know each other. Unfortunately, in the rosy glow of the expectation of getting the job, much is overlooked that can return to haunt you at a later date. It is just like the engagement period before marriage: the more mutual understanding developed, the greater the potential for a happy union.

We were once awarded a government project with a joint venturer selected for us. The early meetings between the firms were delightful lunches, mostly at our office. The one time we went to their office, we waited in a very impressive, large lobby before going to lunch. Since the project was to be erected in the home city of our partner, it was agreed that we would do the design and construction documents and they would staff the contract administration phase. It was only well after the contract signing that we discovered that the two partners of the other firm had only one employee, their beautiful receptionist. The drafting room behind the large lobby was empty! From this experience we learned how important it is to get to know all about your partner, *before* associating!

In the instance where the potential client suggests a firm for collaboration, it's good business sense to investigate the lead. In essence, the client is saying that he has had experience with the other firm and found it capable enough to be considered again for the work. There are other times when the judgment is not as clear, for instance, when the client suggests the firm of a close friend or relative. Here, while the temptation to please is still a factor, the ability of the firm to perform is now your major criterion for judgment. The reason is because the most essential factor to remember is that once selected, the other firm is your partner. It is your team's performance which will determine the success of the project. Usually your acceptance of the partner will relieve the suggesting client of any further obligations. He's all yours. Contractors, consultants, and congressmen are all very good sources of potential joint venture partners.

Contractors, because of their intimate exposure to other companies, are rather skillful judges of the competence and availability of professional firms. Their experience with other firms on a working level can provide you with a good source of information as to the staffing and management of other organizations. However, the information must be evaluated carefully. While the large construction firms have a very broad general view of the professions they serve, sometimes their judgment of an individual firm is warped by their involvement in particular projects in which they might have had a misunderstanding with the design professional.

Consultants, too, have a wide view of other professionals. For instance, large structural or mechanical-electrical engineering firms which serve many architects should have a good understanding of the field. Like the contractors, their knowledge would be gained from actually working with the firms and would have both subjective and objective elements. In essence, regarding the opinions of both contractors and consultants, it will be your task to evaluate the evaluations, finding the "truth" you seek in their advice.

Management consultants are also a good source of information. They have the ability to study and define the capabilities of a firm. Most are also in the field of recruitment. One possibility in finding a partner would be to hire a management consultant to discover a suitable associate for your firm.

Congressmen are included here because they make it their business to know everybody and everything that's going on in their constituency. If you know one, talk to him; if you don't, get to know him.

Other very fruitful sources of information about other firms are your bankers, lawyers, and accountants. They, too, by reason of their services to many firms, may know of capable companies with which you may want to deal. Again, they may provide more "expert testimony" as to the legal and financial aspects of potential partners. The professional skills can best be judged by you alone.

As you can see, the sources of associates are broad and varied. The important elements which you must bring to the selection effort are an understanding of what qualities you are looking for in a joint venture partner and most important, your own desire to associate. The actual choice of partner can come only after several meetings in which an understanding of each other's firm and philosophies is developed.

Interview your prospective associate in the same way that you are interviewed for a project. Examine all aspects of his practice. Discussions must include a full examination of the role of each party in the securing, producing, and staffing the project as well as management and financial relationships. Based upon these discussions and mutual understanding, the decision will be made to joint venture.

CHAPTER FOUR

One Firm's Practice

For the firm that believes in the joint venture way of practicing, the opportunities are limitless in type, size, partners, and clients. Once a successful pattern has been established, the firm develops an interest and a capability which then enables it to seek out the opportunities and provide the know-how to help ensure success. To illustrate the wide variety of venture possibilities available to the interested firm, we include a case history of one firm which has found joint venturing a valid system of practice and, as a result, continues to include joint ventures as part of its total practice.

The firm used as an illustration of this method of practice is Frank Grad & Sons of Newark, New Jersey, now known as The Grad Partnership. The company has been involved in well over 100 joint venture projects of all types. In reviewing the joint venturing history of the firm, one sees how a successful experience can lead to new directions and an expanded scope of practice.

In 1907, Frank Grad founded his firm in Newark, New

Jersey, and during the years leading up to World War II, the firm had the usual architectural-engineering practice, including residential, commercial, and industrial buildings. In 1936, his sons Bernard, an architect, and Howard, an engineer, were brought into the partnership. In 1943, the first opportunity for joint venturing came along. The United States Navy asked the Grad firm to join with Shaw, Naess, and Murphy, Chicago architects, to design a naval ammunition depot at Earle, New Jersey. This project included ammunition-storage facilities, warehousing, railroad and marine installations, and auxiliary structures for personnel. A separate office was set up on the site, and each firm contributed key personnel. Additional manpower was recruited from the locality, and the staff was built up to approximately 175 people.

This experience opened up a new avenue for the firm, and they decided to actively pursue joint ventures as a part of their practice. They found out that the military branches of government were searching for firms to accomplish their work, both at home and overseas. Because of the broad scope and large size of these projects, joint ventures seemed the answer. As a result, in association with engineering firms, the Grad firm formed ventures to design and supervise construction of military bases in many parts of the world, including the United Kingdom, France, Newfoundland, and Pakistan, as well as throughout the United States. Each venture developed an expertise which seemed to open up opportunities to secure other work in the same location or of the same type or scope. Soon the firm became expert at arranging the proper association as well as administering the venture, especially in overseas offices. Using this newly acquired knowledge, the Grad firm went after work in the nonmilitary branches of the government, such as the Post Office Department, the General Services Administration, and state and local governments. Soon to follow was work for large corporations which had building needs similar to those of government agencies, which therefore could be satisfied by the joint venture method of practice.

Meanwhile, the individual practice continued to expand, fed, in part, from the contacts and experience gained from the joint ventures. In 1966, the partnership was increased by six (the author among them). At the time of publication of this book, the firm numbers approximately 130 members and has grown to be the largest in the state. It maintains an in-house staff of architects, using consultants (or joint venture partners) to supply the engineering expertness.

As a result of their successful joint venture experiences, The Grad Partnership recently embarked on a program of establishing subsidiaries, similar to "permanent" joint ventures, to provide entry into new design fields. Joining with Howard P. Hoffman Associates, Inc., corporate real estate consultants of New York City, they have formed a jointly owned subsidiary, GRAD-HOFFMAN, INC., to enter the field of land planning and development for major corporations. This subsidiary operates from its own separate office in New York City, staffed with employees of the Grad and Hoffman firms.

With the Kenneth Walker Design Group, The Grad Partnership formed WALKER-GRAD to provide interior design, space planning, and graphic design services. This separate office is also located in New York City, with employees of both firms contributing to the joint effort.

A third combination is being formed to provide construction management services through the combination of Grad and a large construction company. Each firm will supply expertise during the entire design and construction process. The major effort of monitoring the design phase of a project will be contributed by the Grad office while the construction company will play the major role during the construction period.

In all instances, the various firms in these subsidiaries will continue their own practices.

The idea to enter these new fields and the avenues for implementation were conceived and carried out through formulae developed in the establishment of previous joint ventures. As a result of the careful definition of individual responsibilities, the subsidiary ventures to date have been highly successful.

TYPICAL JOINT VENTURE PROJECTS

The following are examples of some of the joint venture projects of The Grad Partnership (formerly Frank Grad & Sons) to illustrate the wide scope of venturing possible. A picture of the project is included as well as some pertinent information about the venture.

NATO BASES IN FRANCE for the U.S. Air Forces in Europe

Frank Grad & Sons in association with Seelye, Stevenson, Value, and Knecht, engineers of New York City.

This combination added the management talents of the Grad firm to the engineering skills of Seelye, Stevenson, Value, and Knecht. A joint venture office was established in Paris to produce the six air bases. The remote office was managed by Grad personnel from the United States along with lead engineering personnel from New York. Partners from both firms periodically visited the Paris office. In accordance with the client's requirements, the contract documents for this $132 million construction were produced by a French firm of architects, André and Pierre DuFau who acted as subcontractor to the joint venture. The illustrated base at Chalons Vatry, France, is typical of the projects produced by the venture, which accomplished many other military projects together.

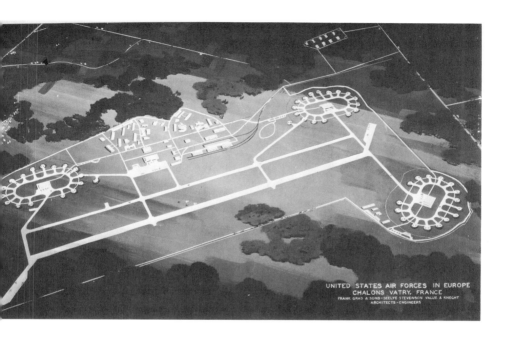

UNITED STATES AIR FORCES IN EUROPE
CHALONS VATRY, FRANCE
FRANK GRAD & SONS—SEELYE STEVENSON VALUE & KNECHT
ARCHITECTS-ENGINEERS

DESIGN OF HARDENED, TACTICAL MISSILE-LAUNCHING FACILITIES at various overseas installations

Frank Grad & Sons in association with Urbahn, Brayton, and Burrows, architects, and Seelye, Stevenson, Value, and Knecht, engineers. Both associate firms are from New York City. The joint venture name was shortened to Grad-Urbahn-Seelye and finally to GUS.

This was one of many military projects with these same partners. A separate office was formed in New York City with lead technical personnel from all offices. Additional men were hired to suit the needs of the project. Grad provided the administrative management skills.

RUTGERS UNIVERSITY, LIVINGSTON CAMPUS, Piscataway, New Jersey

Frank Grad & Sons in association with Anderson, Beckwith, and Haible, architects of Boston, Massachusetts.

The university designated the Boston firm to design the complex which would serve as the first phase of a new campus on the site of the former army camp Kilmer. The preliminary design was accomplished in Boston, and the working drawings, specifications, and construction contract administration were developed in the Grad office in Newark, New Jersey.

THE JAMES FORRESTAL BUILDING, Washington, D.C.

Frank Grad & Sons in association with Curtis and Davis, architects of New Orleans, and Fordyce and Hamby Associates, architects of New York City.

The General Services Administration in Washington, D.C., combined these three architectural firms. A separate joint venture office was established in New York, and the $40 million office building to house functions of the Department of Defense was produced there. The author was the partner in charge of the project, which took a total of eight years from the initial start of the project to the dedication ceremony.

49

NAVAL COMMUNICATIONS CENTER, Norfolk, Virginia

Frank Grad & Sons in association with Marcellus Wright and Son, architects of Richmond, Virginia.

The project consisted of the design of a $7.5 million transmitter, receiver, and control center facility with supporting installations. The work was produced in the Grad office in Newark, New Jersey, with the Wright firm providing local liaison.

51

UNITED STATES POST OFFICE, MURRAY HILL STATION, New York, New York

Frank Grad & Sons in association with Hart, Benvenga, and Associates, architects of New York City.

This architectural association was formed by the Post Office Department in Washington, D.C. The project consisted of a four-story post office occupying an entire city block with a structural capability of supporting a high-rise office building above. The entire project was produced in the Grad office in Newark, New Jersey, by their staff. Benvenga provided periodic review of the documents, and his firm was scheduled to take over the contract construction administration. However, the project was shelved after the completion of the contract document stage.

53

PROPOSED MASTER PLAN, Holland Township, New Jersey

Grad-Hoffman, Inc., a subsidiary of The Grad Partnership and Howard P. Hoffman Associates, Inc.

This proposed 600-acre development for the Riegel Paper Company is one of the many projects produced by this jointly owned subsidiary which was established to provide land planning and development services. The Grad firm furnishes the planning leadership, while the Hoffman organization provides the expertise in real estate market research and financing. The separate New York City office is staffed by both firms and is, in effect, a permanent type of joint venture with both firms continuing their own practice.

GOLF COURSE

N

55

THE NEW JERSEY COLLEGE OF MEDICINE AND DENTISTRY, Newark, New Jersey

Frank Grad & Sons in association with Eggers & Higgins and Gilbert L. Seltzer. Both associate firms are architects and from New York City. The joint venture name is Eggers, Grad, and Seltzer.

The three firms were combined by the Office of Architecture, Engineering, and Construction of the state of New Jersey to design this $180 million complex. Eggers & Higgins were designated "supervising architects" because of their experience in medical school design. To process the work, a separate office was established in New York City, staffed by members of all three firms, with additional staff hired as the work required. Eggers & Higgins are providing the management capability; Seltzer has provided the lead technical man; and Grad, because of its proximity to the site, provided local contact and liaison.

EASTERN AIRLINES NORTHERN REGIONAL RESERVATIONS CENTER, Woodbridge, New Jersey

Frank Grad & Sons in association with J. N. Pease Associates, architects and engineers of Charlotte, North Carolina.

The owner's requirement to design and construct this building within a year's time led to the formation of this joint venture. J. N. Pease Associates had been the architects for a similar building in North Carolina and provided the planning expertise, while the Grad firm added its knowledge of local conditions. The schematic phase was done by the Pease firm in its home office. Upon approval by the owner, the remainder of the project was developed in the Grad home office. Construction contract administration was also provided from the Newark, New Jersey, office. The tight time schedule was met. This is a good example of how a joint venture can provide the "instant expertise" essential in a compressed time schedule project.

59

MASTER PLAN OF NAVAL FACILITIES, Guam, Marianas

Frank Grad & Sons in association with Max O. Urbahn Associates, Inc., architects of New York City and Wall Corporation, engineers of Washington, D.C.

The United States Navy required a master development plan for its facilities on this Pacific island. Included was the design of new housing facilities for other services. A separate office was established on the island to plan the project. The technical effort and project administration were directed by a member of the Wall organization. The Grad office provided the general management as well as leadership in the planning aspects. The key personnel came from the three stateside offices, with the remainder of the manpower imported from the Philippines and other Pacific areas.

60

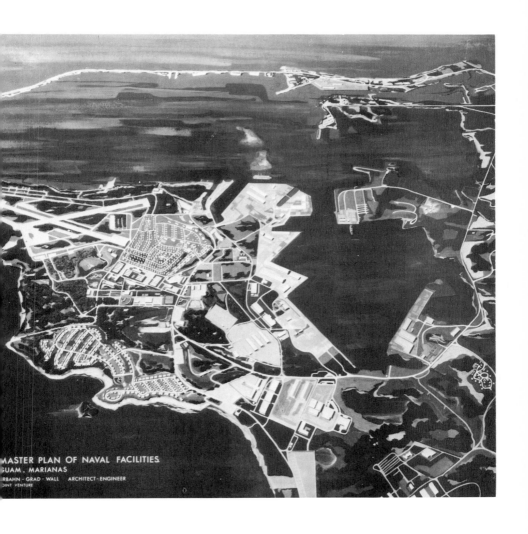

MASTER PLAN OF NAVAL FACILITIES.
GUAM , MARIANAS
RBAHN - GRAD - WALL   ARCHITECT - ENGINEER
OINT VENTURE

61

CHAPTER FIVE

Defining the Relationship

The early and precise definition of individual responsibilities is probably the most important aspect in providing for the success of a joint venture. Yet, despite this fact, these understandings are most often ignored by potential partners. Research has demonstrated that the lack of early definition of responsibilities has led to most of the problems and unhappiness among participants and has resulted in many disillusioned professionals vowing never to joint venture again. And it is to be expected, for there is nothing as painful as learning in the midst of the development of a project that the work which you thought was the responsibility of your partner, he, in turn, was sure was your responsibility. Or the converse, where you expected to handle a portion of the development such as the design, and your associate had the same idea of doing it himself. Not only does this confusion cause professional pain but it also hurts financially as well.

THE FIRST AGREEMENT

The theme throughout this book is the development of a successful relationship during the entire process of the project. The key to this development is the establishment of a precise, mutual understanding prior to proceeding with the project, *well before* a contract is signed with the owner and even before your first interview. It is of prime significance that basic agreement be reached the moment you decide to go after the project. This agreement must be written down and signed by all parties. It may be a simple one page document or, better still if time and circumstances allow, the actual joint venture agreement. However, the form is secondary in importance to the fact that an agreement is established.

It is impossible to precisely define everything before the venture starts. No one can be expected to anticipate everything which will be required during the life of the venture, especially when the commission has not as yet been secured. But, on the other hand, there are many matters which will be inevitably a part of the project. It is these items which should be reviewed and resolved.

How easy it is to neglect these "business arrangements" at a time when the only mutuality of interest is to secure the project. Again the obvious comparison to marriage. It is the engagement period. All parties are on their best behavior. Sweetness and light pervade. The future is a rosy glow. Who wants to talk about the mundane details of division of work, of responsibilities, even of profit? That all will come later. And it inevitably does come in the cold light of reality and usually disillusionment and bad feelings.

The alternative, a *must* for a successful relationship, is the frank discussion of the elements involved, concluding with a written agreement. Do it before the first handshakes are cold and you'll never regret it.

After getting to know everything you can about the other firm's background, experience, and capability, you must give some thought to the project that you are all seeking. It is best to divide the subject into several categories and to analyze each separately. As a result of your discussion and analysis, a written memorandum will be prepared, defining your understanding and agreements in these areas. The following discussion reviews the subjects to be explored during these discussions.

Sharing the Job Development

The first important question relates to how and by whom the sales and promotion efforts will be carried out. The actual techniques will be developed in a later chapter. Your goal now is to define the relative contributions of each of the associated firms in the development of common promotional materials. If there is information about the individual firms already available, thought must be given as to who is in charge of compiling the material into a combined presentation. If new graphic or written material is to be developed for the combined effort, it must be decided who will take the lead.

Another topic which requires discussion is the selection of the person or persons to contact the client and make the presentations. While at first glance this subject may seem simple, it can become complex and involved if not understood. In the case where the client has come from one of the parties who is desirous of protecting his source, without a clear early understanding of individual roles, some unhappy moments may develop. Usually, however, both firms are involved in the client contact and the presentations, since the venture's strength normally depends upon the aggregate of expertise of all firms. The attempt by one firm to "hide" a client from its associates is unrealistic and does not develop among the partners a feeling of trust or mutuality of interest. Frank openness among partners is an essential ingredient to a good relationship.

Another point to be covered in the discussion of the project development is the assignment of one person to be responsible for monitoring the entire job development effort. It is important to select the person and record his name. Similarly a person in each one of the offices should be designated for contact about the project during this promotional stage.

Last, agreement must be reached as to how the expenses for this first effort may be incurred and how they will be shared. In many projects, the amount spent may be small and this issue not of importance. However, troubles usually arise when the expenses mount unexpectedly. This tension gets magnified many times when the promotion proves unsuccessful and the project is not secured. There is an instance where several firms associated to secure a major project in a distant city. During the development period one of the venturers suggested to the others that he retain an attorney to advise on certain legal problems connected with the development. The lawyer was consulted in the name of the joint venture, and because many unanticipated problems arose, the amount of his bill was much more than anyone could have expected. The lawyer's bill arrived after the prospective client announced that the project had been awarded to another firm. No prior agreements had been made between venturers as to the division of expenses. Furthermore, the majority of the matters which the attorney handled related mainly to one firm. To ask all the firms to share in the payment of this unexpectedly high attorney's fee without prior understanding and with no way of recapturing their money put an awful strain on everyone involved. A definite prior decision as to the sharing of costs would have prevented much unhappiness.

Sharing the Responsibility

The division of responsibility during the life of the joint venture can take several different forms, related usually to the relative performance contribution of each firm. It is important at the outset of the venture to determine how responsibilities will be distributed.

Here are some of the forms in which the association can be accomplished:

1. *Each firm assumes the total responsibility for a portion of the work.* For example, one firm develops the architectural work while another firm does the engineering work. Each firm can be given complete authority and, through a mutual indemnification agreement, each firm can limit its responsibility and liability to its own contribution. When the division of the work is so clearly defined, it is possible to clearly divide the responsibility.

However, in the design professions it is quite often not

possible to exactly define the individual contribution of the various members of the venture; therefore, it becomes difficult to assess each firm's responsibility. For example, assume a joint venture of several architects. One is responsible for the design, another develops the contract documents, and the third supervises the construction. Since the development of projects in the design profession is usually a continuum, there often is no precise way to separate the design from the production of contract documents and, in turn, from the administration of construction. Who is responsible for the project cost or time schedule? To whom does the owner turn when he has a design problem in the production or construction stage? When trouble arises in the bidding or building stages, who is responsible? The owner's answer to all these questions must be "the joint venture," but conflict may develop among the parties of the association, each having responsibility for only a specific portion, especially when their income from the venture is likewise directly apportioned to their individual functions.

Despite its potential drawbacks, this method is one most frequently used. To avoid disputes, there must be developed as precise a definition as possible of each firm's duties and responsibilities. In addition, there must be established a viable method of quickly and easily adjudicating disputes arising from the potential gray areas of overlapping responsibilities and interdependencies.

This method has best application in projects where a clear separation can be made between individual contributions to the entire project. For instance, in a design-build arrangement, upon approval and acceptance of the construction documents, the design partner's responsibility ends, and the build partner's interest begins. In this case, this division of responsibility may have additional benefit because it creates a distinct division between the professional and the nonprofessional effort.

2. *The work and responsibility are shared among the participants of the joint venture.* In this method, there is a true partnership developed in which everything is shared. The work load is divided into clearly defined phases and is assigned to one or both parties to perform. The method of assignment is based upon the ability to perform and provide the highest degree of client service.

The contribution of effort is carefully recorded beforehand. With this method, each firm, while not necessarily equal in contribution of effort or in division of profit, fully shares participation in the work, profit, and responsibility from creation through completion. Together all firms operate under clearly defined guidelines of responsibility for performance of each part of the work.

The majority of the ventures in which our firm is engaged conforms to this method of organization, since it is the most flexible and best lends itself to modern management techniques. This is true association from start to finish.

3. *One party takes the position of responsibility and uses the other firm to supply manpower and/or expertise in a specific area.* This particular form is useful where it is necessary to cover the requirements of local laws governing licenses. It also has application where an inexperienced firm has the need for support professionally or possibly financially. In effect, however, this type of arrangement is much closer to a prime-subcontractor relationship, complicated possibly by joint responsibilities to the owner if both firms are cosigners of the prime contract.

A problem which may develop under this arrangement regards responsibility. If something goes wrong, with whom does the liability rest? The firm which did most of the work or the firm which has assumed the contractual responsibility? There seems no clear-cut answer.

4. *Some firms have a continuing loose association with firms of complementary talents, established in order to secure new commissions.* These firms pool their resources and develop common promotion materials. They have a general understanding of how the work will be pursued once the contract is awarded. Until they receive a joint commission, they continue to work independently. Once the project is secured, the organization is established in accordance with one of the above organizational methods.

It must be emphasized that no matter what the form of the relationship, the most important element in the success of a joint venture is the understanding which must be established at the start and reinforced through an agreement recording all aspects of the relationship prior to obtaining the commission.

Dividing the Work

A form has been developed for the assignment of phases of the work that can prove quite handy in the early discussions between partners. This "scorecard" lists the items of architectural and engineering services required for each phase of the work along with the firm having the major responsibility of providing the service (Figure 5–1).

Further, by assigning values to the various services and relating them to the percentage of fee for the particular phase, it is possible to anticipate the percentage of total effort to be provided by each of the parties. If the division of equity in the joint venture is predicated upon the division of work, the percentage of participation can be directly drawn from this chart.

In Figure 5–2, the schedule has been filled out for a venture in which Firm A has the responsibility for architecture while Firm B has the responsibility for the engineering.

A similar form can be created for any other dicipline and combination. The use of this type of form has many advantages. It forces the parties involved to prethink the project, dividing the tasks to be performed and projecting the functional requirements. It allows each firm to anticipate its manpower requirements. It clearly divides responsibilities. It even informs the owner where to look for decision. It also forces both parties to maintain contact throughout the life of the project and, if necessary, pick up and finish the work at any time if the other party is unable to continue.

Our firm has found this chart to be a comprehensive, detailed definition of the work to be accomplished. As such, it has served as a valuable sales tool in a client interview, when the inevitable question is asked, "How and by whom will the work be done?"

This chart is a form of contract between the parties involved and should be included in the actual legal contract, drawn when the project becomes a reality. In this light, the establishment of this agreement must be made with the intention of fulfilling the responsibilities outlined for each of the participants. To this end, each of the parties must take into account the following:

  1. Where one of the firms is specifically given the respon-

sibility for the design of the project, it means that the design decisions are his alone to make, subject to the review of the joint venture management. This particular aspect in the design professions can lead to the greatest potential area of controversy, if misunderstood or given too little thought at the time of this agreement to divide responsibility.

2. The assignment of an area of responsibility to a member of a potential joint venture advises the other parties that the one to whom this activity is assigned will provide the necessary management and manpower to fulfill the assignment in a timely and professional manner.

3. Despite the allotment of a particular area to any one of the partners, the others may have the right of review and comment. The final decision, however, rests with the party given the responsibility.

4. There is nothing which prevents the party not involved in a specific aspect of the work from assisting the party in charge if needed and requested to do so by the latter.

5. Some flexibility in relative responsibilities must occur, since the work outlined in the contract with the owner may contain requirements for services which were not anticipated at the time of establishment of the schedule. When these aspects do arise, they should be added to the chart with responsibilities assigned. A word should be included here about manpower. The design professions continue to have a shortage of skilled and experienced personnel; as a result, there is a tendency to spread the help rather thinly in order to service all the firm's projects. Further, there is an inclination for a firm to favor its own projects over joint venture projects when it comes to an adequate supply of proper personnel. It seems at first glance natural to "favor one's own," especially when under the illusion that your partner will fill in the gaps with men of his own. Experience has shown that this is fallacious reasoning, which can lead to misunderstanding and ill-feeling among partners if allowed to exist. The attitude of each firm in the venture must be that this is its own job to do with the best men that it can supply. When joint venture is compared to individual practice, there is an added note of importance of which all parties must be aware: they have a professional responsibility not

PROPOSED DIVISION OF RESPONSIBILITY
(To be used with AIA Document B-131)

PROJECT:_____   DATE:_____

LOCATION:_____

JOINT VENTURERS: SYMBOLS:

_____ ( )   MAJOR RESPONSIBILITY . . X

_____ ( )   MINOR RESPONSIBILITY . . —

_____ ( )   NO RESPONSIBILITY   . . . 0

% OF FEE	SERVICES	RESPONSIBILITY ( ) ( ) ( )
15%	SCHEMATIC DESIGN PHASE Conference with the Owner . . . . Analysis of project requirements . . . . Assembly of data: Topo and site survey . . . . Utility information . . . . Building code and zoning information . . . . Schematic design studies . . . . Engineering system concepts . . . . Statement of probable construction cost . . . . Development of presentation materials . . . . Presentation to Owner . . . . PERCENT OF FEE	
20%	DESIGN DEVELOPMENT PHASE Conferences with Owner . . . . Refinement of project requirements . . . . Formulation of structural system. . . . . Selection of major building materials. . . . . Preparation of design development documents . . . . Perspective, sketches or models . . . . Statement of probable construction cost . . . . Review plans with applicable agencies . . . . Presentation to Owner . . . . PERCENT OF FEE	

FIG. 5-1

% OF FEE	SERVICES	RESPONSIBILITY ( ) ( ) ( )		
40%	CONSTRUCTION DOCUMENTS PHASE			
	Conferences with the Owner			
	Architectural working drawings and specifications			
	Structural working drawings and specifications			
	Mechanical/electrical working drawings and specifications..........			
	Preparation of bidding forms			
	Update of statement of probable construction cost			
	Assistance to Owner in filing with government authorities			
	Presentation to Owner			
	PERCENT OF FEE			
5%	BIDDING OR NEGOTIATION PHASE			
	Conference with the Owner			
	Preparation of addenda			
	Response to contractors' questions during bidding period			
	Negotiation with successful Bidders..........................			
	Assistance in preparation of contracts			
	PERCENT OF FEE			
20%	CONSTRUCTION PHASE			
	Preconstruction conference			
	Shop drawing checking and approval:			
	Architectural			
	Structural...			
	Mechanical/electrical			
	Material approvals			
	Site visits			
	Change order procedures			
	Approval of requisitions and issuance of payment certificates			
	Issuance of progress reports			
	Final inspection			
	Final acceptance			
	Administration during guarantee period......................			
	PERCENT OF FEE			
	TOTAL			

PROPOSED DIVISION OF RESPONSIBILITY
(To be used with AIA Document B-131)

PROJECT: _POST OFFICE_

DATE: _APRIL 9, 1971_

LOCATION: _SYRACUSE, N.Y._

JOINT VENTURERS:

SYMBOLS:

A.B. SMITH ARCHITECTS (A)

MAJOR RESPONSIBILITY . . X

JONES ENGINEERING (B)

MINOR RESPONSIBILITY . . —

_____ ( )

NO RESPONSIBILITY   . . . 0

% OF FEE	SERVICES	RESPONSIBILITY (A)	(B)	( )
15%	**SCHEMATIC DESIGN PHASE**			
	Conference with the Owner . . .	X	—	
	Analysis of project requirements . . .	X	—	
	Assembly of data:			
	Topo and site survey . . .	X	0	
	Utility information . . .	0	X	
	Building code and zoning information . . .	X	0	
	Schematic design studies . . .	X	X	
	Engineering system concepts . . .	—	X	
	Statement of probable construction cost . . .	X	X	
	Development of presentation materials . . .	X	0	
	Presentation to Owner . . .	X	—	
	PERCENT OF FEE	10	5	
20%	**DESIGN DEVELOPMENT PHASE**			
	Conference with Owner . . .	X	—	
	Refinement of project requirements . . .	X	—	
	Formulation of structural system . . .	—	X	
	Selection of major building materials . . .	X	0	
	Preparation of design development documents . . .	X	X	
	Perspective, sketches or models . . .	X	0	
	Statement of probable construction cost . . .	X	X	
	Review plans with applicable agencies . . .	X	X	
	Presentation to Owner . . .	X	—	
	PERCENT OF FEE	12	8	

FIG. 5-2

% OF FEE	SERVICES	RESPONSIBILITY		
		(A)	(B)	( )
40%	**CONSTRUCTION DOCUMENTS PHASE**			
	Conferences with the Owner	X	—	
	Architectural working drawings and specifications.	X	O	
	Structural working drawings and specifications	O	X	
	Mechanical/electrical working drawings and specifications.	O	X	
	Preparation of bidding forms	X	—	
	Update of statement of probable construction cost	X	X	
	Assistance to Owner in filing with government authorities	X	—	
	Presentation to Owner	X	—	
	PERCENT OF FEE	23	17	
5%	**BIDDING OR NEGOTIATION PHASE**			
	Conference with the Owner	X	—	
	Preparation of addenda	X	X	
	Response to contractors' questions during bidding period	X	X	
	Negotiation with successful bidders	X	—	
	Assistance in preparation of contracts	X	O	
	PERCENT OF FEE	3	2	
20%	**CONSTRUCTION PHASE**			
	Preconstruction conference	X	X	
	Shop drawing checking and approval:			
	Architectural	X	O	
	Structural	O	X	
	Mechanical/electrical	O	X	
	Material approvals	X	X	
	Site visits	X	—	
	Change order procedures	X	O	
	Approval of requisitions and issuance of payment certificates	X	O	
	Issuance of progress reports	X	O	
	Final inspection	X	—	
	Final acceptance	X	—	
	Administration during guarantee period	X	—	
	PERCENT OF FEE	12	8	
	TOTAL	60	40	

only to the client in this case, but also to the other members of the group.

Another factor affecting manpower is the size of the joint venture project. Because this system of association is used most often for very large projects, it is quite likely that a firm's share of the project will be very large in comparison to the size of the other projects in the office. As a result, manpower should be apportioned on this relative basis.

Financial Arrangements

It is just as important to have a prior understanding among the parties about the sharing of the finances as it is to have a preliminary agreement on the division of technical effort. Without exception, the only correct time to agree on the subject of money is before the project is started.

The preliminary agreement regarding finances has three major aspects: the arrangement for funds during the period of promotion, the provisions for funds from inception of the project until the first payment, and the division of profit or loss during the progress of the project. During each of these different periods, the division of effort will vary, and therefore, the financial arrangements should be explored.

Sharing Development Costs

As described earlier in this chapter, the understanding regarding the division of costs for the promotion of the project is important, especially when the efforts to obtain the commission prove unsuccessful.

There are several ways to divide the development costs, depending upon the conditions involved. Here are some of the methods which have been used:

1. If the effort involved in the promotion is relatively equal among the parties, then each partner expends the time necessary for his contribution and absorbs the cost of this effort as part of his own firm's promotional expenses. This method is the least complicated and is used most of the time where no unusual effort or expenditure is involved. In these instances, the contribution of the partner's time is the major ingredient in the common promotional effort. The required

record keeping is nonexistent, or at most insignificant, with each partner monitoring his own firm's efforts.

2. Where there is likely to be a pronounced inequality among the partners in the promotional effort, there must be developed a method of sharing the costs, usually in equal shares. Each firm assigns a separate project number to the work and keeps track of the time and costs expended. At the end of the effort, whether successful or not, the costs are added and then divided by the number of firms, and each firm pays its respective share. An interesting question arises here. How should a firm charge for the time expended in the effort? A usual method of charging a client is through a multiple of direct labor costs, in order to cover overhead and profit. Should this same formula be used to cover the development expenses of a potential joint venture? The answer can be anything the partners agree upon. We have found it best in our practice to exclude any charge for profit in determining these costs. We usually form an agreement to charge an agreed-upon multiple, such as 1.8 to 2.0 times direct labor, to cover office overhead. The profit will come from the project if the promotion is successful. There are situations, however, where the charge for profit would seem justified. If one of the partner firms takes on the major role in the promotion and, by reason of its small size or the size of the effort, is required to expend the effort of a large portion of its staff for a significant period, then there should be some consideration of providing compensation including profit to the firm, in order to replace the income lost from its normal practice during the promotion period.

3. Where the promotion effort is likely to involve considerable direct expense the sharing of the costs is usual. We have been involved in ventures in which it was determined that the best method of securing the commission would be through the development of extensive printed material, such as a combined brochure. The cost of designing and printing this document was considerable and was borne equally, through previous agreement, by all partners. In another development the travel expenses to the remote site of the client were shared by all parties. The method of payment is usually through billing after the effort has been expended,

similar to method 2 above. We have found it impractical to set up a "kitty" in advance with the various firms contributing, since there is no real joint venture entity to administer the fund.

There is no reason why the sharing of the costs should be on an equal basis. Where there is a joint venture being formed in which one firm is assigned a much larger share of the profit to be realized from the venture, there is a basis for that firm to pay the larger share of the development costs, since this firm has most to gain by the success of the selling program. In most cases, the same firm has the larger proportion of the sales effort. There are many ways to determine the method of sharing promotion expenses. Each special case should receive its own analysis and solution. However, to avoid controversy, the important element is to record the agreement in advance.

Sharing Profit or Loss

An important financial decision, which must be made at this early stage, is the relative sharing of the profit and loss which result from the operation of the joint venture. Again, this agreement must be made before the commission has been awarded. There are two basic methods for apportioning the interest in the venture:

The Fee Split   The total fee for the project is split into agreed-upon percentages. Each member firm does the work assigned to it and absorbs the cost of this work. Its profit from the venture is whatever is left of its portion of the fee, after subtracting its expenses. The general costs of the venture, such as joint venture stationery, legal fees, etc., are apportioned to each firm in accordance with the fee-split percentages.

The Profit Split   The total fee for the project is held by the joint venture. Each member firm is reimbursed by the venture, in accordance with an agreed-upon formula, for the services it performs on behalf of the venture. The general costs of the venture are paid from the common account. Once all costs have been expended, the remaining profit is split into agreed-upon percentages.

The fee-split method is advantageous when a fairly exact definition of effort can be established. Each firm can take its part of the work, almost as a separate project, with its profit in direct relationship to its own efficiency. Problems arise, however, because of the overlapping areas which often occur in a project. The solution of these problems directly affects the profit picture of one or the other of the firms; consequently controversy may arise more quickly. In contrast, the profit-split method allows all to share the costs and the profit much more as a "partnership," thus avoiding the direct conflict of individual firms' interests. We have found the latter method much more desirable and have used it almost exclusively in recent years.

In both methods, usually, the relative percentage of equity in the venture is directly related to the amount of effort which the individual firm must expend in the operation of the venture.

There are other factors, however, beside the ratio of effort, which may determine the relative financial positions of the partners. For instance, one party may bring to the joint effort a unique quality, such as a close relationship to the client, which may be the key to securing the commission. Just like the factor of technical effort, this ability to "get the job" has definite value to the joint venture. A discussion among the partners will establish both the relative value of this contribution and the equity positions of all the partners.

Another factor which will have a bearing upon the establishment of relative equity positions in the profit-split is the method in which reimbursement is made to each firm for the effort which it has expended on behalf of the joint venture. Chapter 8, which describes the operating procedures of the venture, reviews this subject in detail. Generally, however, if the method of compensation for effort that is established includes a factor for profit on the direct labor expended in the effort, then the division of the monies remaining in the joint venture account may be done on a basis different from one established purely on the relative ratio of effort. This would be justified since the parties will already have received profits based on their relative efforts.

In a joint venture in which many disciplines participate,

it is sometimes very difficult to equate the effort involvement of all the parties. For instance, finding a basis of comparison among such disparate activities as those of a contractor, a financier, a real estate consultant, and a structural engineer is rather complex. However, each must be compensated for his participation, and some agreement at this early stage must be established. It takes mutual understanding, patience, and often a lot of negotiation, but it must be done. It hopefully establishes a pattern of cooperation which should last throughout the project.

From our experience, we have found that the best relationships result where there is an equal sharing of interest, whenever it can be practically employed. This method seems to eliminate one of the biggest problems to which joint venture members are subject, jealousy about each other's financial interest. Many times, even though our effort might have been calculated at a slightly higher ratio than our partner's, we still have suggested an equality of position, in order to forestall possible future problems.

Additional Agreements

Other areas, which should be covered in the preliminary discussions among potential partners, can be almost as important as the decisions regarding technical effort and financial relationships. These additional topics for review include: where the work will be done, how the work will be done, and miscellaneous matters of agreement.

Where the Work Will Be Done   This decision can have a profound effect on the operation of the individual office, should one be selected. For the large office, where the new project represents a small percentage of the effort, the effect of the decision about where to locate the joint venture is minimal. The impact, however, on a small office when it suddenly receives a new, large job can be startling if not properly provided for. For instance, personnel from the other firms suddenly "invading" the office and employees freely trading information about benefits, salaries, and other working conditions may cause a morale problem. So the decision about "where" can have unexpected side effects.

It has been our experience that it is best on smaller joint

ventures to do the work in the home offices of the participants, each doing his share with his own men. For instance, if we are doing the architecture and our partner the engineering, we each work simultaneously in our own offices. If the project is very large, however, with the potential of severe impact on the home offices, the decision has always been to establish a separate office manned by contributions of personnel from the several partner firms. This arrangement has the added advantage of establishing for the joint venture effort a separate overhead that is unaffected by the varying overheads from the several home offices. Another reason for the establishment of a separate office is a possible advantage of being close to the client or the site. For that reason we have had offices variously in such locations as France, Guam, Newfoundland, Pakistan, Thailand, and other remote areas. However, before any decision is made about a remote office, a review must be made of the problems of supplying home personnel or recruiting new personnel to man the new office. Matters such as living allowances, wives and families, tax considerations, etc., come into play. So the decision to open a foreign base of operations is not one to be taken lightly. Chapter 9 will discuss this matter.

How the Work Will Be Done   This is the time to agree generally on the type of organization which will turn out the work. Of basic importance at this time is who will participate in the positions of leadership and control. This ranking starts from the top. Which partners of each firm will participate? Who will be their alternates? Who will have the day-to-day control of the work, and what system of control will be exercised? These are questions which must be discussed at this stage. If possible, it is best to name the individuals who will participate in the various roles of responsibility.

Miscellaneous Matters of Agreement   There are other items to discuss and decide upon at this time. The name of the venture is an area which can later cause friction if there is no prior understanding. Usually, the name of the joint venture is "Firm A and Firm B, associated architects," where there is an almost equal sharing of the responsibility. Whose name comes first may be decided alphabetically, or by the flip of the coin. Where there is one firm which has the distinct leadership position, the name can be listed as "Firm A, supervising architects, Firm B and Firm C, consulting architects." Where there are many firms involved, a new name can be established from a combination of the names, such as GUS, a joint venture of Frank Grad & Sons, Urbahn, Brayton & Burrows and Seelye, Stevenson, Value, and Knecht. Another method is to pick a name associated with the project and list in the subheading the names of the participating firms. For example, Newark Center Architects, a joint venture of———. A note of caution in selecting a name: check your state registration laws to see what is allowed.

Other items which warrant discussion at this time concern the choice of the major consultants to the joint venture. You should include not only the technical consultants but also your attorney, your accountant, and, in some instances, who will do such work as public relations or blueprinting.

The distribution of correspondence and information during the promotion period is worthy of review at this time. Who is to be "copied in" can become a "sticky" subject, especially when a participant has been left out of the distribution of an important piece of correspondence.

The absolute importance of developing and recording these prior understandings cannot be overemphasized. The more items discussed and agreed upon at this early stage, the easier the venture will flow during its operations. Especially is this true when there are more than two parties involved or when they are new to each other. The success of the venture will be a direct result of the scope of mutual understanding gained during this "engagement" period.

CHAPTER SIX

Getting the Job

The selling of services is a process which varies greatly with the many different circumstances and individuals involved. Each firm's approach to securing commissions is unique and changes in response to the demands of the particular project. Much that is helpful has been written about the techniques of marketing professional services. However, the methods of promoting a joint venture project have certain unusual qualities which are worth reviewing.

SELLING YOUR SERVICES

The goal is to develop the most effective sales effort which the combination of firms can produce and thereby obtain the commission. As in any new business promotion, the main effort is to convince the client that the skills your group has qualify it, above all others, to answer the needs of the project. As in any other type of organization, there are both positive and negative characteristics which must be understood in order to provide the best picture to the client. In the pro-motional effort, naturally, the "plus" items will be stressed, while the "minus" items will be played down. However, the venture must have some valid and ready responses when the client asks about the less favorable aspects.

Positive Areas of Emphasis

The joint venture brings together firms of broad spectrum and/or depth of skills. Further, the combined experience of the participants is usually much greater than that of a sin-gle-firm competitor. Thus, the first positive area to stress is the skill and strength of the total organization. This asset includes the greater dimension of the available manpower, both technical and administrative.

The fact that the combination of skills has been chosen in direct response to the needs of a particular project reinforces the proposition that you possess this strength in the special-ized talent required to produce the work.

This basic statement of strength must then be supported by a demonstration that the organization has been established to apply this strength to respond to the specific needs of the project in the most efficient manner. The client must feel that the several firms which form the venture have been melded together to form a well-oiled machine to do his work.

Negative Aspects

The prime problem in selling a joint venture is the question of the ability of these several firms to work together as a single unit. The owner many times feels, and sometimes from bitter past experience, that, in having the temporary combination of several firms perform the work, there is a great risk that their efforts will be inefficient and uncoordinated. He sees himself losing money and time and ending up with a poorly designed project.

To offset this feeling, the joint venture must demonstrate that it has the ability to fuse the diverse elements into a smoothly operating, efficient new machine. To foster this confidence in the mind of the potential client, the venture must prove that the new combination is not just the sum of several firms, but much more; that the effect of gestalt takes place, where the result is greater than the sum of the parts. Or, in mathematical terms: $1 + 1 = 3$.

In developing a joint promotional effort, a major problem to be overcome is the sense of competitiveness which the parties to the venture have developed throughout the years of their own practices. It is now imperative that the participating firms forget their past competition and each bring to the common effort a sense of full participation and candidness. Sources and secrets as they pertain to the common goal must now be revealed. This is truly the test of the cooperative spirit which must pervade the entire life of the venture in order for it to be the most successful.

CONTROL OF THE PROMOTIONAL EFFORT

The decision of several firms to attempt to secure a joint commission can best be brought to a successful completion if they follow the same principle which they apply to their own individual practices: there must be one central point of control of the promotional effort. A principal from one firm should be chosen to monitor the development from beginning to end. The participation of all firms will be subject to his direction. Within each firm he will have a contact person who will be able to respond, in a timely manner, to the requirements as they arise. It is important that the "team captain" remember the necessity of keeping all parties informed of the progress of the effort. Copies of all correspondence should be circulated to all firms. The basic program for the development should first be established in a joint meeting where all partners contribute their expertise.

The actual promotional effort, while directed by one person for maximum efficiency, is rarely the work of one man or one firm alone, except in cases where one partner firm is able to bring in the job. Normally the contributions of all firms are necessary in both technical help and participation at partner level. Nothing can match the sales power of the coordinated abilities of the several member firms. This strength, in fact, is one of the major advantages of the joint venture system.

Joint Presentation Materials

The specific project will determine the type of response necessary. The simplest way of forming a joint presentation is to pool the materials of the several firms. Assuming that it is a government project you are after, all firms could supply their own GSA 251 forms which could be stapled together and sent with a covering letter to the government.

An alternative to this method would produce a much stronger presentation without much additional effort. This option would involve the retyping of the information on one combined form that represents the entire venture, with the manpower statistics listing the sum of all the firms' capabilities. The experience portion similarly is the result of combining the major projects of all firms and, as such, is a much more impressive display than two or three different forms. A cover listing the name of the new venture should also be included.

The presentation now becomes identified as the product of a new entity, the joint venture. The emphasis is on the combination, not on the individual firms, which continue, however, to play the "subtheme" to the main "melody."

In the preparation of joint graphic materials, an important aspect must be the sense of uniformity and continuity. For instance, a combined slide presentation should be selected so that while the broad scope of experience is demonstrated, the slides are fairly uniform in size and quality. This should be accomplished even at the expense of having to duplicate or remake some of the slides. We had the experience in which our regular slide presentation was on standard 2×2 inch slides, while our partner used super slides. To assure uniformity, the selected slides were remade in the larger size. Similarly, black and white photographs used in a combined brochure should be of the same size and quality. With the development of new, inexpensive, and easy-to-use binding techniques, it has become a much easier task to combine materials from several firms into a common presentation brochure. We have had excellent results using the transparent-acetate envelope pages to insert photographs. In addition, typed pages of biographical material and other background information are all combined into a booklet through the use of plastic binders. The covers are attractively done with colored paper and rub-on lettering, with an acetate top sheet for protection.

An especially important aspect of any joint venture graphic presentation is the organization chart. One of the most usual questions which the client wants answered is how this new combination of skills, which in many instances has never functioned together before, will combine to function efficiently on this project. The chart which is prepared should indicate graphically what has already been decided by the partners in their previous discussions: how and by whom the job will get done. The chart should show which firm has been assigned the various duties and responsibilities necessary to complete the work of the contract. In as many instances as possible it should list the name of the actual person who will perform under each of the major titles. This chart can do much to demonstrate to the prospective client that the venture has anticipated the project problems and devised a method for their solution. Through the use of colors the chart can demonstrate the contributions of each firm, which blend together in the common effort.

All correspondence on behalf of the joint venture in the promotion effort is most effective if it is written on stationery created for the venture. This is a minor expense, compared to what is to be gained by successfully obtaining the commission, as well as being an effective demonstration to the client that your group is a viable, substantial, and serious unit, prepared to render services. In designing this stationery, it is usually advantageous to create the image of a new entity with an identification of its own. The logo for the venture should therefore be of a different design than that of any of the member firms. This same new logo should appear on as much of the material submitted as possible.

In some instances, where the expense is justified by the prospect of the goal to be achieved, extensive promotional materials can be jointly prepared. The joint venture for one project in which we were engaged decided, based upon one successful experience, to go after another major project. To produce the best graphic product to represent the joint venture, we hired a graphic consultant to develop a brochure aimed at securing the new project. The basic approach was to show how well the joint venture had worked in producing the first project and how they could apply the same skills, background, and experience to work on behalf of the new commission. Since both projects were government office buildings, there was a logical sequence. The product of this effort was a large brochure, 12½ × 16 inches, with 32 pages of biographical information, background, experience, and information as to method of operation and an organization chart.

DEVELOPING CONTACTS

As in your individual practice, an important element is the development of your contacts who might have some bearing on the selection process. In the case where several firms are going after the job in a joint effort, the pool of contacts can be appreciably larger. In simplest terms, it would be in everyone's best interest for each member to contribute his contacts to the joint effort and thereby provide it with the greatest thrust. What happens in practice, however, especially when the several firms are normally operating as competitors, is a reluctance to provide some names to the other parties and thereby lose possible future competitive advantage. In this event, each joint venturer must analyze his individual situation and his obligations to his coventurers as well as to his own firm. If he can possibly contribute his contacts' names to the joint effort, he should do so. However, if this is not possible, he still might be able to develop a specific contact for this particular project in the name of the joint venture, without revealing the identity of the contact to his associates. While far from the most efficient method, at least it lends help to the venture while still preserving the contact for the firm.

We have found an interesting phenomenon in connection with the pooling of contacts. Often, because of the interrelationship between the various names contributed to the joint effort, new contacts arise because of mutual friends, business associates, relatives, etc. Again the synergistic effect of the joint venture.

The Joint Presentation

Most large projects seem to require the personal appearance of key members of a firm for an interview. This requirement stems from the increasing use of committees or boards that are charged with the selection of design professionals for the project. Their actions are subject to the scrutiny of either the public, in the case of governmental commissions, or the corporate hierarchy in the case of private work. With their deliberations and decisions in general view, they require the credibility of personal appearances of principals and the documentation of the presentation to reinforce their verdict.

For the joint venture group, the personal appearance at a selection interview creates certain unique problems, which must be recognized and overcome in order for the group to be successful. The joint venture representatives must be aware that one of the strongest objections which the potential client seems to have against employing a joint venture is the concern that the collection of firms will not operate as a unified group. The client fears that his time and money will be wasted while the members of the venture learn to work together in an efficient manner. It is against this objection that the joint venture must focus its special attention during the presentation. The object: to gain the potential client's confidence that the team created is not only the most technically competent but also the best organized of all the firms being interviewed.

An important method of demonstrating technical skills of the venture is through a description of the previous successful projects which relate to the type of project being sought. This should be the easiest part of the presentation since the very basis for the combination of the several firms was to provide the depth and range of skills necessary for the particular project. An important consideration is the development of the required material in a form which establishes a feeling of uniformity, as if produced by one entity. This feeling of common identity is established through such simple devices as the repetition of the joint logo or the use of the same type-writer or colored paper.

This same theme of "singleness" must be reinforced by the organization and personnel you present. First, the organization required to produce the work must be carefully thought out in advance of the interview. Where appropriate, a chart of organization which clearly shows the various components and flow of work and responsibility should be displayed. In addition to this chart, wherever possible, principals of each firm should be present at the interview. Beforehand they should have carefully reviewed the assignments of tasks to their various firms and be prepared to speak authoritatively on their own parts of the work. We have found it important at these meetings that the partners elect one "team captain" for the interview who will start off the presentation, introduce members of the venture, and field all questions, passing them on to the partner of the appropriate discipline as they occur. Not only does this method allow for the most efficient way of responding to questions, but also, more importantly, it demonstrates to the prospective client that partners of the joint venture firms are individually interested in the project as well as collectively able to work successfully together.

Very often, during the interview, the request is made to identify the actual people who will be involved in the project. While this question is not unique to a joint venture, its special significance lies in the way that the team responds. The client continues to look for the demonstration of consistency and organization at all levels, and most importantly at the operating level. We have always made it a practice, wherever possible, to have present at the interview the actual people whom we would propose to do the job. Again, one man, preferably the man who will actually lead, "quarterbacks" the working team, involving the other members where appropriate. The importance of constantly reinforcing this theme of smooth organization cannot be overemphasized.

Another technique we have found successful during the interview is the use of name plates. Because of our desire to present as many members of the venture as possible, we found that we usually had quite a crowd representing us at the meeting. This can become difficult to the members of the interviewing committee, who must struggle to remember all the names. What we have done to overcome this problem is prepare in advance identifying name plates which are placed on the table in front of each individual. Again, these name plates are uniform in appearance and contain the logo for the joint venture. It is surprising how a simple device such as this is appreciated by your clients, especially if your interview is one of many they hold that day.

Within this main theme of "togetherness" there is an important subtheme of "individuality" which should be evident at the presentation. The beauty of your joint venture is that you have gathered together the best firms in the different fields needed to respond to the project's requirements. The best analogy is an orchestra. Each individual musician is an expert at what he does. All together they create beautiful music. Similarly, the emphasis in your presentation is that you have created a viable organization of these firms, a positive, unified combination with carefully conceived management and organization, not a segmented temporary arrangement.

THE FOLLOW-UP

Just as in individual practice, the postinterview follow-up is important. Proposals made verbally during the interview should be confirmed in writing. Each partner must now employ his contacts. Any additional material should be forwarded to the client, always using joint venture stationery. One name and address should be left with the prospective client for his further contact.

Should the verdict be negative and the project awarded to another firm or association, it is always helpful, if at all possible, to learn why your group did not receive the commission. This information might be of value in your future presentations. For instance, if the information were received that a certain member of your joint venture was thought to be weak in the area of expertise for which he is proposed, the possibility may develop that you will want to substitute a stronger member in that discipline, should you find a similar opportunity in the future. While many times it is difficult to obtain a clear and honest evaluation of the reasons for the selection of another firm, wherever this information is obtainable, it is worthwhile seeking.

On large projects which attract many proposals, the chance of being successful is reduced by the size of the competition. A newly formed joint venture which is unsuccessful in its early attempts to secure work should not be discouraged. The more the members of the team meet and develop presentations together, the smoother their operation and understanding of each other. This growth in understanding and a corresponding ease of working together will become evident to prospective clients and will eventually assure success in the development of new work.

The remainder of this book will be based upon the assumption that your group has been successful in gaining the commission and that the joint venture you have formed will now proceed to produce the project.

CHAPTER SEVEN

The Joint Venture Agreement

As in any major undertaking involving more than one participant, the first step is to consummate a legal agreement recording the understanding among the parties. No matter how
small the undertaking, no venture should proceed without
this agreement, since it forms the legal basis for the interaction of all participants. It is similar to the understanding
which must be developed among partners in a newly formed
partnership. As described in Chapter 5 it is best if this agreement is developed before the contract with the client is signed.

   In the development of this contract, all parties should be
represented by their lawyers. After the initial discussions,
usually one attorney will draw up a draft of the agreement
and then circulate it to all parties for their review and suggestions. Because of the unique quality of every joint venture,
by reason of its different participants as well as the varied
scope of the work to be performed, there are as many different joint venture agreements as there are joint ventures. In
addition, the American Institute of Architects has developed,

with the aid of the author, its own standard form of agreement. A draft of the document is included in Appendix C of this book. Copies of this document, when approved for final publication, will be available from the main office of the AIA in Washington, D.C.

Appendix B of this book includes a copy of a typical joint venture agreement between an engineer and an architect, used by the author. It was developed prior to selection by the client. The actual agreement for a specific project must be prepared by the participants' attorneys specifically for the particular project. For example, the agreement in Appendix B is based upon the fact that there is a separate document, such as is contained in Appendix A, which describes the main operating procedures.

This chapter will discuss various aspects of the more important paragraphs usually included in a typical agreement. There is no attempt to cover every aspect of the agreement, but rather to highlight some major points. The ideas covered result from the specific experience of the author and are not to be taken as suggested solutions or legal opinion, both of which should come from the advice of qualified attorneys.

TYPICAL PROVISIONS OF THE AGREEMENT

The first part of the agreement usually identifies the various parties of the joint venture and, where partnerships are involved, lists the names of all partners. In the case of corporations, the names and addresses of the officers who ratify and adopt the agreement on behalf of the corporation are included.

The project is then described in as much detail as possible, indicating the general scope, location, name of client, and a description of the agreement entered into by the joint venture with the client. Since this contract with the owner forms the basis for the entire undertaking, quite often a copy of this contract is attached to the joint venture agreement.

It is important to note that often, especially in the case of government contracts, there is language in this prime agreement which must by law be placed in the joint venture contract. For example, the requirement for nondiscrimination in employment is something which the joint venture as a unit itself guarantees the owner, and, in turn, there must be a binding agreement among the venturers on this point.

After a description of the undertaking, in the following sections mutual understandings as to other aspects of the work are recorded. The following paragraphs are neither a complete list nor a proposed order of arrangement, but rather some suggestions as to areas worth covering in the agreement.

Rights of the Parties

Usually this paragraph simply states that the terms of the agreement will govern the relationship and the actions of the various parties in the development of the work required by the contract with the client.

Name of the Venture

This paragraph records the name which has been agreed upon by the venturers. Before deciding on the name to be used, the parties should request that their attorney familiarize them with the requirements of the state laws which will have jurisdiction over the venture. In many states, the use of names, other than those of the participating firms, is prohibited. In fact, some states do not accept firm names allowed in other states; they require the individual names of the professionals actually licensed to practice in their state to appear alone. For instance, a firm of architects named Smith, Jones, and Brown practices in one state, but the venture is in another state whose laws allow only those registered in that state to appear on documents. Brown might be the only one of the three partners licensed to practice in that state, and therefore only Brown's name may appear in the venture's name.

Normally, the individual firm names are listed in an agreed-upon order. However, often a simple name can be derived from the first letters of the various firm names, or from several syllables; thus GUS was created from the firms of Frank Grad & Sons, Urbahn, Brayton & Burrows, and Seelye, Stevenson, Value, and Knecht. The joint venture name for the firms of Eggers and Higgins, Frank Grad & Sons, and Gilbert L. Seltzer became Eggers, Grad, and Seltzer. Other firms use combination names such as "Joint Venture Architects" or "Associated Architects and Engineers." Another common practice is to use the project name as part of the name of the venture, such as "King Building Associates" or "Medical Complex Joint Venture." Usually, after the list of the firm names, the words "associated architects (engineers)" appear in the name in order to designate the form of the undertaking.

Interests of the Joint Venturers

If the decision is to divide the fee of the project among the parties, this paragraph simply records the percentage (or lump sum) division of the fee.

If the profits or losses will be divided among the participants, then the agreed-upon method will be recorded here.

Since there are many methods possible for the division of equity interest, the language of this paragraph may vary greatly, from a one-sentence description to distribution through a complicated formula. The common methods of equity assignment include the following:

Fixed Percentage Division   The most usual formula is through a fixed percentage division to all the parties. This option has the advantage of being the easiest to describe and administer while creating the fewest problems. The different percentage for each of the parties is arrived at through negotiation and agreement.

Actual Work Load Percentage   When the sharing of profit is dependent upon the sharing of the work load, the division of profit and loss will be established at the end of the venture, in proportion to the actual effort expended on behalf of the venture by the individual offices.

The usual method of measurement is to calculate the proportion of each home office's direct technical payroll paid in connection with the project compared to the total direct technical payroll incurred by all offices in the development of the work. For instance, if Firm A paid its technical staff a sum of $50,000 for work on the joint venture's account and Firm B paid its staff a total of $30,000 and Firm C paid $20,-000, then the total direct technical payroll would be $100,000. The individual proportionate shares of participation in the profit would be:

Firm A   50%
Firm B   30%
Firm C   20%

However, when the firms are from different parts of the country and when there is a large disparity between the prevailing salary and wage rates, a special provision may be put in the agreement which will modify the computation of the division of the net profit to equalize this disparity. For the sake of interim distribution during the course of the project, interim percentages are established and payments made based on this ratio. At the completion of the project, adjustments are made to be consistent with the final percentages.

Division by Stages Another method involves relating the interest of the different parties to the income accrued or loss incurred in the different stages of the work for which each is most responsible. For instance, if the function of one is to develop the preliminaries of a project, that firm might be accorded the larger share of the profit derived in that stage and a smaller share of the profit derived in the other stages of the work. For clearest definition, the stages of the work should be the same as appear in the contract with the client. Some problems occasionally arise from the employment of this method, however, and they should be carefully analyzed beforehand. For example, there was a joint venture of three architectural firms, one of which was designated the supervising architect because of its intensive background in the specific type of project. Because the supervising firm would be doing the major portion of the schematic phase of the project, it proposed a complicated "interim fee" of varying percentages for each phase of the work. There was, in addition, a final equity percentage at the completion of the project. The formula read as follows:

Phase of Work	Paid Percentage	Interest of Partners, %		
		Supervising Architect	Architect A	Architect B
Schematic	15	95	2.5	2.5
Design development	25	40	30.0	30.0
Contract documents	40	36	32.0	32.0
Construction	20	33.3	33.3	33.3
Overall fee at completion	100	45	27.5	27.5

The paragraph in the contract included the following stipulation:

> Notwithstanding the interim distribution of profits or sharing of losses made in accordance with the above schedule, it is understood and agreed that subject to an audit of the joint venture accounts after the conclusion of the project, the distribution of profits and losses for the entire project shall be in strict accordance with the proportions listed in Paragraph 6 (45% — 27.5% — 27.5%) and that appropriate adjustments shall be made as required to achieve this result.

It seemed like a rather complicated but workable formula until several problems began to appear. For example, the standard form of agreement between the joint venture and its engineering consultants stipulated that the percentage paid to these engineers (of their fee) for their work in the schematic and design development phases be smaller than the percentaged joint venture's fee from the client. This was based upon the fact that engineering consultants expend less effort than the architect during these preliminary phases. However, in the contract documents phase, a larger percentage of an engineering consultant's effort is utilized. The comparison was this:

	Percentage Received of total Fee		
Phase of Work	Joint Venture	By Structural Consultant	By Mech/ Electrical Consultant
Schematic	15	8.38	5
Design development	25	15.28	20
Contract documents	30	45.8	45
Construction	30	30.54	30
Total	100	100	100

The problem arose in computing the profit for each phase, since the interim percentages of the partners varied with the phases. For instance, when calculating the profit to be divided at the end of the schematic phase, the expense for the engineering consultants could be based upon the amounts actually paid in accordance with the consultant agreements (8.38% to structural engineers and 5% to mechanical engineers) or the consultants' fee for this stage could be accrued at the same fee percentage received by the joint venture from the owner (15%). This difference in percentages can make a considerable difference in the profit calculated for a specific phase. The same is true at the contract documents phase in which the consultants are receiving a greater percentage of their fee than the architect receives. Should this phase be penalized by the heavier payments due, by contract, to the consultants?

Another complication which can result from the same type of varying interim-percentage arrangement has to do with excess income tax which may be paid. Suppose, using this same example, that the schematic stage showed a profit of $100,000 while the succeeding stages broke even. The firm getting 95% of the schematic-stage profit would have to show its share of this profit ($95,000) as income and would have to pay tax on this income. With the succeeding stages showing no profit, the end profit of the venture would be this same $100,000 which, by contract, would be shared in the proportion of $45,000 for the supervising architect and $27,500 to each of the architects A and B. The supervising architect, having paid taxes on an income of $95,000 would now be declaring a loss of $50,000. However, what about the interest lost on the taxes paid several years ago?

Furthermore, if the money had been distributed, the supervising architect would have had to dig into his pocket to return the difference.

Division by Split Arrangement   In some ventures, a split arrangement is established. For instance, the parties may agree to an equal sharing of the first 10% of the profit (or loss) with the remainder distributed in direct ratio to the amount of effort, as described above.

Experience has demonstrated that the simplest formula is the best and easiest to administer. No matter what method, it must be carefully conceived and exactly defined.

Supervision of the Joint Venture

The agreed-upon procedure allowing the principals of the various firms to exercise their control over the operation of the venture is described here. This control is exercised in various ways, depending upon the amount and type of effort which the various parties will expend in turning out the work. The most efficient procedure which we have found in the many ventures in which we have been involved is the establishment of a policy and operating committee, which is described in greater detail in Chapter 8.

It is important that this paragraph in the contract name the representatives of the firms who will collectively exercise the necessary controls, identifying the manner of voting and assigning to a specific individual any special power of decision which may be agreed upon.

One of the duties which should be assigned to the policy board is the naming of a project manager and a business partner. Their major duties should likewise be listed. This paragraph of the contract should also include provisions for alternate representatives only when the principal representative is absent or incapacitated or unable to serve. A decision must be made as to whether the representatives will be paid by the venture for their participation in the policy committee. Opinions differ as to whether principal's time in the function of administering the project should draw hourly compensation or should be paid from the profits realized from the venture. The problem arises when there is a greater contribution of effort from one or two principals while the others "go along for the ride." We have found a sound compromise in the establishment of compensation for principal's activities in the administration of the venture. There is no payment to any of the principals for attendance at meetings at which all firms are represented. If, however, any firms are not represented, by reason of absent delegates and alternates, then those remaining principals attending are compensated for their time in accordance with an agreed-upon rate. Furthermore, travel expenses are reimbursed to all parties to avoid penalizing the distant venture firm.

Another stipulation that frequently is inserted in this section of the agreement states, in effect, that none of the members of the policy board shall be liable to the joint venture by reason of their actions as such, except in the case of grossly negligent or actual fraudulent or dishonest conduct.

In its exercise of full responsibility and authority over the performance of the undertaking, the policy board includes decisions on such matters as assignment of work between the various venturers, preparation of the schedule of the work, settlement of disputes with the client, and the appointment of the key operating personnel. Much of the definition of responsibilities may have already been established through the use of a form similar to that found in Chapter 5. This form should be included in the agreement.

A question which must be resolved and clearly spelled out in the agreement is whether a unanimous or majority vote will be necessary for the actions of the policy board. No matter what the decision, the actions and decisions of the policy board must be final, conclusive, and binding upon the joint venture.

Other provisions which are sometimes inserted in this portion of the joint venture agreement are such things as:

1. The requirement that written minutes be kept of all policy board meetings and that they be signed by all members in attendance.

2. In circumstances where meetings of the policy board are not convenient or feasible, decisions may be made in lieu thereof by written memoranda exchanged between the authorized representatives or by exchange of letter.

3. For all decisions, in lieu of a unanimous vote, where one firm has been given a specific responsibility, such as to lead the design effort or to provide the engineering skills, this firm may be given the right to overrule the others in the specific matter of responsibility.

Financing of Services

In this portion of the agreement, the financial arrangements are made. Decisions must be made and recorded on the many money matters which will affect the smooth operation of the association.

A bank account or accounts must be opened in the name of the joint venture. Usually, the policy board will decide on which bank will receive the venture's business. Decisions must then be made as to the amount and assessment of the initial deposit to start the undertaking, before any fees are received. These amounts are quite often listed in the agreement. Usually, the contributions are in proportion to the percentage interest of the parties. Each firm must designate the individual or persons who is authorized to sign on its behalf. The policy committee may determine how many signatures will be required on the checks.

In some joint ventures where there are large sums involved, a system of several accounts may be set up, with the control from the larger savings account to the smaller checking account accomplished through the several signatures required for withdrawal.

When additional funds are required, as determined by the business manager, the member firms are required (within a stated number of days) to forward the amounts necessary, in proportion to their percentages of interest. When a joint venturer is unable to pay, then the others usually make up the deficiency; payments, including interest, are returned when sufficient fees are received.

Where there is an excess of funds, amounts may be distributed in accordance with the schedule of percentage of interest. In addition, payments are made on a periodic basis to the firms actually doing the work. This is accomplished upon the receipt of invoices to the joint venture from the firm supplying the manpower and accomplishing the work, all in accordance with the agreed-upon markups as described elsewhere.

Stipulations must be made in the agreement regarding the services of accountants and attorneys performing services on behalf of the venture. The costs of these services are to be borne by the venture, including the cost for the preparation of the joint venture agreement itself. Usually, the policy board is empowered to select the professionals who will render these services.

Books of account are kept in a manner (accrual or cash, calendar or fiscal) and at such place as designated by the policy board. An independent audit is usually provided for A statement to the effect that the certified figures of the auditor selected by the policy board shall be final, conclusive, and binding upon the joint venturers can be extremely beneficial in the resolution of disputes which might arise.

If the joint venture agreement is drawn up in advance of obtaining the work, or if such an arrangement is determined by the parties, a paragraph covering the distribution of the preliminary expenses in the development of the prospect, up until the time of the signing of contract with the owner, may be of importance. These travel and other out-of-pocket expenses, upon agreement, may be considered a part of the cost of the undertaking and may be paid out of the joint venture funds. If the promotion is unsuccessful, the agreement dictates the method of sharing the expenses.

In addition to the reimbursement of technical personnel performing work on behalf of the venture as described in the next chapter, a careful definition is in order as to what constitutes direct expense which will be reimbursed to the joint venturer at cost. These items usually include telephone and telegraph, travel, reproductions, models, recruitment expenses, overtime meal allowances, and allowed entertainment costs. The basic contract with the client may determine other areas of reimbursement.

Other Provisions

The following are stipulations which most often are found in the joint venture agreement:

Disputes and Arbitration This provision sets up the procedures for the adjudication of controversy among members of the venture. Of importance among parties from various states is to list the arbitration procedure as well as the state in which any legal proceeding will take place.

Default of a Joint Venturer This clause covers what happens if one of the parties withdraws or defaults. Stipulations must be made as to how the work will proceed as well as how the profits or losses will be distributed at the conclusion of the work. It must also guard the surviving venturer(s) from interference from creditors, etc., during the life of the undertaking, usually stating that any required distribution to claimants be made at the conclusion of the venture. Moreover, a clear definition must be made of what shall constitute a default under the contract.

Relationship of the Parties   This clause generally describes the fact that the relationship between the joint venturers is a temporary association limited to the performance of a specific contract, and will not have any continued association, limitation, or liability beyond this specific undertaking unless agreed upon.

It allows the various parties to continue to carry out their own business affairs at the same time as the joint venture is in operation. Quite often a group of firms will continue a loose association arrangement in the anticipation of securing other work as a joint venture.

Another item of agreement which falls under this paragraph includes the understanding that should there be extensions, modifications, additional contracts, or future follow-up work for the same client, sought in behalf of the joint venture, the work shall be done jointly and not by the individual firms. On the other hand, language could be included to allow individual firms to do work for this client on smaller, or local, or specialized projects, without interfering with the mutual obligations among the parties.

Indemnification   In some agreements, especially where there is a clear definition of the individual responsibilities of the various parties, a clause may be inserted which protects the individual firm from liability arising from the failure of any of the other parties in the performance of their work. Even if the operation of the joint venture is covered by professional liability insurance, this paragraph in the agreement may protect the individual firms from the others' liability with regard to the deductible amount. In addition, it would provide protection beyond the term of the insurance.

The following is a typical indemnification clause of the type which might be included in a joint venture agreement:

> If, as a consequence of the negligence of any member of the joint venture, the other members of the joint venture sustain liability not covered by insurance, the negligent member of the joint venture shall indemnify and otherwise hold the other members of the joint venture harmless against such liability.

Death or Withdrawal   The continued operation of the venture under the conditions of death or withdrawal is described in this clause. Usually, upon the death of one of the partners of one of the joint venture firms, one of the remaining partners of the firm which sustained the loss would carry on for his departed partner. The problem arises, when one of the firms is a sole proprietorship, as to who will carry on representing that firm. Various solutions are possible, depending upon the particular circumstances, ranging from the withdrawal of the firm from the venture to the establishment of the right of the executor of the deceased partner to appoint a new principal from the staff of the deceased member's firm to carry on, subject to the approval of the surviving venture members.

Miscellaneous Provisions   Many joint venture agreements contain paragraphs listing more specific and detailed understandings than are contained in the sample joint venture agreement in Appendix B. Some of these items are:

1. Describing the exact method of reimbursement for the work of the joint venture firms, similar to the description contained in paragraph III (3) of Appendix A.

2. Listing the names of the joint venture's attorney and accountant.

3. Stating the number and names of those whose signatures are required on checks drawn against the joint bank account.

4. Inserting a paragraph regarding public relations to the effect that all public statements and releases must contain the name of the joint venture in an approved form of identification and these statements must be cleared through the policy board.

5. Listing the type and amount of insurance for each participant to maintain.

6. Inserting a paragraph on noncompetition which specifically prevents any of the parties from soliciting work from the owner for a definite period from the date of termination of the basic agreement with the owner. Usually excluded is the situation in which the owner offers work to one of the

parties, without his prior solicitation, provided that this party notifies all the other joint venture members.

7. Including a list of specific services each of the parties is to perform.

8. Listing the specific property each of the parties is to contribute.

9. Defining the circumstances under which a joint venturer may or may not act unilaterally.

All of these provisions are certainly valid considerations for agreement. However, we have found that often the detailed information in regard to these items is not available at the very outset of the project. These agreements then become a matter of operating policy developed by the policy board and listed in an operating procedure. The requirements for definition of detail vary with the parties and with the project. Your attorney is in the best position to advise you on your specific requirements.

For each individual joint venture, there must be tailored a special agreement, taking into account the specific requirements of the work to be performed under the basic contract as well as the individual requirements of the firms comprising the association. Handshakes and verbal understandings are not enough. It must be a written instrument, prepared by a competent professional.

CHAPTER EIGHT

Organizing the Project

After the legal and financial relationships among the joint venturers have been defined through the joint venture agreement, the framework of organization must now be established to produce the project. Since an almost endless variety of possible joint venture combinations results from the different mixtures of participants as well as different sizes and scopes of projects, it would be impossible to list all the variations of organizational structures possible to turn out the work. However, there have developed through the years several types of organization which are most typical and which would apply to the majority of joint ventures among design professionals.

OPERATING PROCEDURES

Before starting any project, a common procedure is to record the method of organizing the project. This written memorandum becomes a part of the agreement and serves as the pattern for the future functional relationship of the venture. A typical example of this type of document is included as Appendix A.

CONTROL

No matter what organizational structure is decided upon to produce the project, the joint control of the effort by all participating firms is essential. One of the best methods to achieve the necessary supervision is through the creation of a policy and operating committee composed of principals of all the firms involved. These partners meet periodically to review all major aspects of the project. Usually an equal vote is given to all parties; however, when there is a large disparity between the interests of the various parties, the vote may be proportionate to the division of equity. It is of utmost importance that the members of this group find the time to attend the required meetings and to decide upon various items brought before them in a timely manner, thus avoiding unnecessary delay in the progress of the work.

While ordinarily all partners should pass judgment on all aspects of the venture, there are instances where the collective judgment of all principals is not indicated. For example, in the type of venture where one firm is given the responsibility for the design of the project, the policy committee may discuss all matters of the project, including design, with the final judgment in design matters left to the firm assigned that responsibility. Similar reservations may be made for any other aspect of the venture which has been assigned to the jurisdiction of one party. However, it must be realized that when all parties share the responsibility for the successful completion of the project, for their own protection they should have the right to review and pass judgment on the major aspects of the work.

In addition to the policy and operating committee there must be a chain of command to produce the work. A partner or associate of one firm is usually placed in charge of the operation. In instances where the work will be done in several offices, the project partner will change with the phase of the work. It is the responsibility of the partner in charge to provide a constant flow of information to the other members of the venture to ensure that they have been kept up-to-date on important events. It has proved to be very helpful for the policy and operating committee to choose a business manager, usually a partner from one of the firms, who will follow and advise on all problems related to the financial matters of the venture. He may, in turn, use his own controller or others in his own office for any assistance he may need.

As in almost every project, the actual operating head of the venture is the project manager. He has the continuous supervision of the entire work. However, in a joint venture, even more than in an individual office project, this man is the key to the success of the project. He must have not only the technical know-how and ability to get along well with the client, but also a sensitivity to the individual requirements of the members of the several firms involved. He must possess the ability to resolve irritating issues that sometimes arise. He must have a talent for diplomacy. Even when a project is to be done in only one of the offices, or in several consecutive offices, it is important to have one project manager, preferably a member of the firm who will have the greatest responsibility for the production of the project.

The project manager reports to the partners through the policy and operating committee. In the line of command below this project manager are the various people necessary for producing the work. Illustrated in Appendix A is the organization chart for a joint venture of three architectural firms on a large building project.

Other Methods of Control

If circumstances are such that the above control method is unworkable, there are many other ways of organizing the project. Where one aspect of the project, such as the design, is the sole responsibility of one firm, it is possible for that firm to control the project, on its own, through that stage of the work. The design would be done in this one office as if it were the firm's own project. At the conclusion of this phase it would be turned over to members of the "production office" for their development. Each firm would have an administrative responsibility to inform the other firms of the progress

of the work and other important matters. This loose arrangement might be necessary, for instance, if the parties to the
venture were geographically remote from each other, or if
the disciplines involved in the project were extremely varied.
However, since each of the various parties to the venture must
share the responsibility for the other's work, the importance
of communication and review with the other partners cannot
be overstressed. Despite fairly large geographical separations
between members of ventures in which we have participated,
we still have found it invaluable to hold periodic meetings
among partners of all firms in order to jointly review the
work. Not only does this aid communication, but also it
provides a pool of expertise which is the very basis of the
strength of the joint venture.

At other times it may be the decision of the joint venture
partners to elect one member to represent them as a decision
maker. This method is a practical solution either to the
venture composed of firms separated by long distances or
for the venture set up in a foreign country. Naturally, it is the
responsibility of the one man "committee" to keep his partners
informed of all major decisions. Further, he must have the
sensitivity to know when to call a meeting of all partners to
decide on matters which he feels beyond his own scope of
individual decision.

No matter which method of organization is decided upon,
it should be set down in writing, preferably in a separate
document, so that all members of the association will be
aware of the individual duties and responsibilities.

PERSONNEL

The ensurance of an adequate supply of capable manpower
in the effort is one of the factors critical to its success. Basically two categories of manpower must be supplied, technical
and administrative, which are normally furnished by the
home offices to work in either the home office or a common
joint venture office.

It has proved generally desirable for the joint venture not to
have a payroll of its own, since this involves additional

bookkeeping and records. When there is a requirement for the venture to have additional manpower, this is generally accomplished by having one of the home offices hire the new man on its staff and then supply him to the joint venture. This has a further benefit of attracting more and better men, since they are being hired by existing firms which create a greater sense of permanency than the temporary venture. Further, employee policies such as vacations, sick leave, and other benefits have already been firmly established for each firm. It is usually best to spread the assignment of newly hired personnel as evenly as possible among all the offices so that they share the burden.

Where a separate joint venture office is established and the agreement calls for an approximately equal effort and participation by all the firms, there should be a method set up to assure this goal to the best degree possible. The project manager should be given the responsibility to call on the various offices to supply manpower as required by the progress of the work. He should review the manpower situation from time to time as to number and suitability. He should have the authority over all personnel assigned to the project. At the discretion of the project manager, personnel considered unsuitable will be returned to the home offices. This rule is basic to the smooth operation of the venture.

In order to minimize the impact of the joint venture activities on the home offices, it is important that the manager project his manpower requirements as far in advance as possible, thereby giving the home offices as much lead time as possible. The same is true about the return of personnel to the home offices.

It is also important that the home offices, when providing men, realize that they are supplying the manpower on a permanent basis, not to be retrieved when a crisis arises at the home office. If someone is to be supplied on a temporary basis, that understanding should be clearly developed between the home office and the project manager.

A more detailed discussion of the manpower aspects of the joint venture is contained in Chapter 10.

Financial Arrangements

The financial aspects of the joint venture must be carefully controlled so as to avoid undue unhappiness among the partners. In this regard it is best to consult with a knowledgeable accountant who can advise the venture what procedures to follow. As in the other aspects of the venture, there are several possible arrangements. This book will describe a number of arrangements which have proved successful in the past.

One of the first steps is to appoint an accountant to prepare the financial statements for the venture. Usually, the firm serving one of the partner firms is chosen. In this regard, it is important to choose a firm which has had some experience in the preparation of reports for joint ventures, since there are a few aspects of accounting that are peculiar to the joint venture method of operation. In addition to the appointment of the accounting firm, it is sometimes wise to provide for an independent auditor to audit the books at periodic intervals. It is also helpful for the accountant to be located near the office in which the joint venture bookkeeping will be done.

The accountant shall determine the form and detail required for the invoices submitted by the various home offices. Usually these invoices are submitted on a monthly basis. They are reviewed and approved by the project manager before payment is made.

The choice of which firm will keep the books and records is quite often based on which firm is likely to have the largest share of the activity. However, we have found that a more important measure of who should do the bookkeeping is based on which firm has the spare capacity and leadership to provide the necessary services. It should be recognized that the record-keeping and bookkeeping requirements of a sizable venture can match that of a medium-sized office and the firm taking on these responsibilities should be prepared for the task ahead.

The method of reimbursement for the effort of each office in the development of the project may vary considerably, depending upon how and by whom the work will be turned out as well as the fee arrangements with the client. Generally, the joint venture reimburses the home offices for the use of personnel on the basis of a multiple of the hourly technical rate paid to the employee. It is the determination of this multiple which varies considerably and determines in large measure the basic approach of the partners to the sharing of income. In this regard it is best to examine the different categories of personnel involved and the various arrangements.

Principals   While the income for principals or officers is usually derived from the profit developed by the venture and is distributed to the member firms, in order to recognize special effort, the principals are usually compensated for direct effort in behalf of the venture on the basis of an agreed-upon, flat hourly rate applied equally to all. The work involved may be technical or administrative, but the rate would be constant. A distinction should be made, however, in evaluating the administrative time which is chargeable. It must be direct administrative time to the venture, not related to time involved in such matters as:

1. Discussions or reading of technical and administrative correspondence necessary to keep current with the development of the project.

2. Considerations of home office personnel to be assigned to the joint venture or reassigned to a home office.

3. Any other subject which does not relate to *direct* administrative effort.

In addition, quite often the principals agree not to charge for the time spent in attendance of policy and operating committee meetings when members from all firms are present. This device has a twofold effect in preventing a rapid depletion of the cash as well as serving as a measure to help assure participation by all members of the venture at these important policy meetings.

A list of names of those who fall within the category of partners or officers should be prepared and included in the memorandum of understanding or the agreement. When a new man is made a partner of one of the participating firms, he does not go on the joint venture list without the approval of the policy committee.

The active participation of the partners of a firm in the joint venture is to be encouraged, since the success of the venture may well depend upon their guidance. However, it must be understood that the chief source of income to the home offices will be in the division of the profits developed throughout the project, rather than the payment for a principal's services on an hourly basis.

Associates   The compensation for the direct effort of associates or junior officers is made on a basis similar to that of payment to principals. The hourly rate is established (usually lower than that of the principal's rate), and payment is made on account of the actual hours spent in the direct technical or administrative effort. Again, there must be a list prepared, identifying the names of the associates of each firm who will participate at the rate specified.

When an associate from one of the firms is given the responsibility for the full-time direction of the venture in all or any of the stages of development of the project, then a special arrangement as to salary may be made, or he may be paid on the same time-factor basis as applies to the other full-time technical employees who contribute effort to the project. In addition he may be the recipient of a special bonus paid to him by the venture at the end of the project, or he may be granted participation in the profit resulting from the operation. In any event, special consideration should be granted to these key employees.

Technical Personnel   When technical work is done by an employee of one of the joint venture firms, the home office employing the man can expect to be compensated for the time spent by this employee. The most usual form of compensation is by a multiple of the man's direct technical salary. The factor which is used in establishing the multiple varies greatly in different ventures. An analysis of the various factors which must be considered in establishing this multiple is worth considering.

This method of compensation is based primarily on the hourly wage of the employee. The various offices present to the venture's bookkeeper a roster of employees who will be working on behalf of the venture, listing the hourly rate for each employee. It is important for all firms to periodically update this roster, keeping it current with the hiring of new employees and the raising of salaries. In some instances, in lieu of the actual hourly salary per employee, a rate for each category might be established and compensation returned to each home office on the basis of this uniform list. For example, junior designers may be compensated at the rate of $3 per hour and intermediate designers at the rate of $4 per hour, etc. While this method may tend to make the bookkeeping easier, it is hard to imagine other advantages of this system weighty enough to offset the obvious disadvantages of attempting to categorize individuals of varying talents. Further, this method has the inherent risk of underpaying men from higher-salaried offices and a consequent reticence to provide the proper manpower. As a result, most usually it is the employee's actual salary rate that is used.

Normally, adding the following items to this rate will result in full compensation for effort: the payroll burden, "overhead" costs, and profit. Just as these factors are taken into account in determining the fee in the private work of each firm, so, too, do they play a part in the determination of the internal financial arrangements of the joint venture.

The salary burden is the amount of money each firm must pay to support the efforts of the individual employee. In addition to the federal and state payroll taxes, it includes sick leave, vacation time, and payments made by the firm for medical and other insurances. The amount paid will vary with the policies of the individual office in terms of what employee benefits are standard. In establishing the joint venture policy of reimbursement to the home offices for technical effort, it is usually best to set one standard rate to cover salary burden. In ventures in which we have been engaged, we have used figures varying from 15 to 20% of direct payroll for this item. However, with employee benefits rising all the time, 20% may soon be too low.

The payment for "overhead" is usually the most controversial of all the factors discussed. Overhead expense refers to all the other expenses necessary to run an office, such as telephone, legal and accounting costs, drafting and office supplies, insurance, etc. As a result, the home-office charges to the joint venture for these expenses will vary, based upon where the work is actually performed. If the work is being accomplished in one of the home offices, then the rent, insurance, telephone, supplies and equipment, etc. for that home office are being expended for its own practice plus the joint venture work. It is impossible, therefore, to isolate the overhead costs for the venture project. If, on the other hand, the work is performed in a separate joint venture office, then a separate and distinct overhead cost pattern is automatically established by the actual expenses.

In this regard, there has been a lot of discussion among accountants which leads to the conclusion that the total overhead of a joint venture operating from a combined office cannot be measured solely by the expenses of the separate office. To these expenses, these accountants maintain, there must be added a portion of the home-office overhead, since the removal of the employee to the remote office does not reduce the office expenses of the home office to any great extent. The rent, telephone, equipment, leasing, and other expenses still continue undiminished. In fact, by reason of the departure of the employee, the home office becomes less productive and therefore less efficient. As a result the overhead factor, applied to the lower direct technical labor cost, increases.

Another factor, which will influence the overhead percentage to be reimbursed on account of the technical labor expended, is the cash flow of the project. It is often necessary, in order to have sufficient funds in the operating account of the project, to limit the amount of funds paid to the partner firms during the course of the project. One way of doing this is to keep the overhead factor low, at a percentage that represents near actual cost. The remainder of the compensation will be distributed at the conclusion of the project, in accordance with the equity interests to the partners.

Our firm has found it best to follow the principle just described, limiting the reimbursement to the member firms during the progress of the work to the lowest possible amounts. As a result, we have found the following method of distribution to be successful in most cases:

For Technical Personnel
1. In the home office . . . . Salary plus 85 to 100%
on straight time (this covers
both salary burden and
overhead costs)
2. In the joint venture
office. . . . . Salary plus 20% on straight
time (this covers salary
burden costs)

In both instances, only salary is paid on premium time.

By following this practice, the payments during the development of the venture are reduced to the smallest amounts necessary to cover home-office costs, thereby preserving the cash balance until the end of the project. Where an excess of cash builds up, a distribution is made to the partner firms in accordance with the equity interests stipulated in the joint venture agreement. It is important to note that whether or not distributions are made, under income tax regulations, each partner will be taxed for his proportionate share of the joint venture's income. However, once the tax is paid, any later distribution of these retained profits is tax-exempt.

Clerical Personnel   The payments to the partner firms on account of clerical work done for the joint venture project present a different problem. Since this category of work is normally classified as part of the support or overhead costs, it is not usual that an additional overhead factor be added to the salary cost. There are, however, the payroll-burden costs which the joint venture home offices must assume for the personnel involved. As a result, it is rather standard practice to add only a payroll-cost percentage, such as 20%, to the straight-time salary of clerical personnel, whether they are in the home office or a separate joint venture office. For premium time, only salary is paid.

Other Methods of Compensation

In addition to the financial arrangements described above, there are other possible formulas which respond more directly to specific conditions of a particular project. The basic goal of any financial arrangement is the equitable distribution of funds to compensate the individual firms for their efforts on behalf of the common endeavor, while preserving enough cash in the venture to pursue the work. In the following paragraphs some other possible methods of financial organization are discussed.

In the venture in which each firm has a specific responsibility to shoulder, it is possible to allocate the finances on a basis directly related to the technical effort. For instance, if Firm A is given the responsibility for the design, then the funds received for the design stage are the payment to the firm. Similarly, Firm B which produces the contract documents will be entitled to the fees derived from that stage. However, since there are some expenses which apply to the work of the entire venture, such as bookkeeping, legal fees, accounting costs, presentation costs, etc., a fund must be set aside by all the participants to cover these expenses. To accomplish this in an equitable manner, a percentage of the income for each phase can be allocated for these common costs. This method of separation of income by stages of work performed has the apparent advantage of isolating the different efforts and rewarding the efficient firm for its work, while penalizing the poor producer. However, it has the disadvantage, as described earlier in the book, of segmenting the operation, thus creating tensions among partners. This is especially true if one phase is a loser while others are winners, because it is often so difficult to accurately separate all the factors of the various stages.

Another rather common method of distributing payment for effort is through the use of a higher multiple of technical labor. In cases where it is difficult to determine in advance the percentage of contribution which each of the firms will expend, reimbursement for effort could be based upon a multiple factor which would include salary burden, overhead costs, and a portion of profit. For instance, in lieu of the salary plus 85% for technical work in the home office, under this system the rate might be salary plus 125%. Similarly, instead of salary plus 20% for participation of personnel in the joint venture office, the formula in this method might be salary plus 60%. Under this system most of the income will be distributed as a direct result of the individual office effort contributed; therefore, this system should reflect more accurately the profit distribution because of its direct relationship to the particular participation of each different office. A prior agreement must establish the percentage distribution of any remaining funds of the venture. This final distribution may also be based on the ratio of the actual payments to the individual firms, again reflecting each firm's degree of participation. The problem may be one of keeping enough cash in the till to permit completion of the work without necessitating borrowing from the partner firms to replenish the working capital.

This method has also worked successfully when the prime contract with the owner is based on a multiple of direct labor. In this case, the multiple used for distribution to the partner firms should be smaller than that received from the owner, so as to maintain a cash reserve. For example, if the owner is billed at 2.5 times direct personnel expense (direct technical labor plus, let's assume, 20% for payroll burden), for each direct payroll dollar there would be added 20 cents for salary burden to make it $1.20, which is then multiplied by 2.5. Thus the billing for $1 of labor will be $1.20 \times 2.5 = $3. For payment to its own members on account of work accomplished, the venture may elect to pay salary plus 125%. Thus for each $1 in technical labor expended, $3 would be billed by the venture, and $2.25 would be paid out to the firm doing the work. The remaining 75 cents would remain in the bank account to pay for the common joint venture expenses, including reimbursement for administration expenses which are not billed to the owner, such as bookkeeping, partner's participation, etc. This last financial arrangement described above can only operate successfully if the work is accomplished in the various joint venture offices and not in a separate office, since the expenses of the separate office would require that a much greater reserve account be maintained in order to satisfy the expenses.

Correspondence

Another aspect of organization which deserves careful attention is the establishment of a smooth flow of communications among the partner firms. Procedures must be established at the outset of the project for the control and dissemination of correspondence and information. There are three basic categories of information which must be distributed: technical, administrative, and contractual. Each category has its own "need-to-know" aspects which should determine its routing. The following is a discussion of some of the procedures which we have used in our past ventures.

Technical In general, the dissemination of technical information is confined to the personnel dealing directly with the technical phases of the project. The project manager is the focal point of control for this type of information. His primary objective, in the reception and distribution of technical material, is the efficient completion of the work. However, his secondary objective must include keeping the policy and operating committee current with changes to the program, due dates, meetings, review comments, and any other items of significance which could affect the decision-making capabilities of the committee. The business manager must be kept informed of any matters which may affect the business and financial structure of the project.

Where the project is carried out simultaneously in several offices, the duplication and dissemination of technical data take on added significance. Each firm must be kept knowledgeable about the other's activities and decisions. Further, when a project will be produced in a series of consecutive offices, a technical record must be maintained and transmitted with the project from one office to the next.

When the project is produced in one separate office, complete files will be maintained in that office. However, the responsibility still remains with the project manager to distribute information to all parties who need to know about the particular subject.

Administrative Matters of a general administrative nature are usually handled by the project manager. It is his responsibility to see that the various members of the joint venture are informed, usually through the policy and operating committee, of all important administrative aspects of the project. Copies of important letters and memos dealing with administrative subjects are to be circulated to all offices.

Contractual   This category is a special division of administrative material which requires restrictive handling. The principle of "need-to-know" should be strictly observed. The material which falls within this category usually includes: agreements with the owner and consultants (particularly portions dealing with fees), cash statements, income projections, calculations for extra fees, salaries, invoices, distribution of income to home offices, and any other matters dealing with the financial arrangements of the venture. The business manager of the venture is the one who usually determines the distribution and handling of specific correspondence in this category.

Whenever possible, all correspondence, reports, transmittals, and other written communications should be typed on stationery and forms prepared especially for the joint venture. While for the smaller ventures it may not seem worth the expense to print separate stationery, it is by far the best way to handle the joint venture correspondence. Whether the letters or reports emanate from separate offices or a combined office should have no impact on the decision to use separately printed joint venture letterheads. All correspondence of any kind should be identified by the proper firm name, that of the joint venture. When there is no separate joint venture office, the address might be the several home-office addresses of the venturers with "please reply to:" identifying where return correspondence is to be sent. Potential problems may arise when a letter is sent to the client under the logo and letterhead of one of the partners. It may not only cause problems among partners, but also confuse the client who is looking to one separate entity, the joint venture, to produce the project.

The types of joint ventures are numerous, in both the variety of the participants as well as the scope of the projects. To attempt to describe one organizational setup which will respond to the needs of all combinations is impossible. The organization of this type of association is really no different from that of the organization of a single office. The only aspect that is more critical is the development of methods of joint control and the establishment of clear lines of communication and authority. Once this is done to the satisfaction of all parties, the operation of the venture should run as smoothly as any major project in an individual's office. In fact, it may run more smoothly, since there will be others with whom to share the problems. In fact, they probably will be able to suggest solutions which are not apparent to the individual practitioner.

CHAPTER NINE

Producing the Project

The manner and method of developing the work should not differ appreciably under a joint venture association from that of a project developed under private practice. Obviously, the technical requirements for a project will remain the same. However, there are several important aspects of a joint venture organization which make it unique in the way the work is developed. The challenge is in taking advantage of the positive aspects of the joint venture, while anticipating the areas of potential conflict.

As described throughout this book, there are many valuable assets in the joint venture type of organization which can yield considerable advantages in the way that the work is accomplished. After the job is procured and the legal and accounting matters have been determined, it is now time to take advantage of these benefits in developing the project in the most efficient manner.

There are many decisions which must be made in determining the manner and method of producing the work. The following is a discussion of some major categories for decision, with a review of the various elements to be considered. At the outset, it must be emphasized that because of the many different combinations of projects and participants, there is no one right way to do things. This chapter will develop the various alternatives available and discuss the relative merits of each. The decision as to what method is best for a particular project must rest with the participants choosing the options they feel are best suited to the circumstances of the project.

LOCATION

Where the project will be produced can have a considerable effect on the cost, time, and general efficiency of the work. One of the advantages of a joint venture is that you have several options which can be exercised in the selection of the site of operation.

The first basic decision is whether the operation, or any part of it, will be done in a separate office or in one or more of the individual offices. In general, it is best if the project is turned out in the offices of one or several of the joint venturers, since it avoids the necessity of finding and leasing new premises as well as the problems of furnishing and staffing a separate operation. In projects where the fee is split and each venturer is responsible for a specific part of the project, it is almost always accomplished in the individual offices. However, this is not practical when the job is large in size or scope and necessitates an infusion of many men into the home office of one of the members; then the adverse affect to the home office can more than offset the advantages of the separate office.

Using the Home Office

If the work is to be turned out in the office or offices of the participants in the venture, many positive factors accrue. Mainly, these advantages result from the economies possible through the sharing of facilities as well as the minimum of disruption to personnel.

If the joint venture project is small or if, as is the case with many projects, slow periods are encountered, it is possible to schedule the personnel of the office so that they work on private work during the slow periods. This arrangement prevents wasteful, idle man-hours from penalizing the joint venture project manpower costs. Furthermore, through the use of the individual offices, a similar sharing of the overhead costs with the private practice can be accomplished by splitting on a pro rata basis the cost of such items as insurance, secretaries, accounting personnel, office boys, etc.

Another advantage of the use of the home office for the production of the whole or part of the work results from the fact that, under this system, displacement of technical personnel may be held to a minimum. The men will be working in their own offices, at their own desks, all in familiar surroundings. This has a great psychological value which affects the efficiency in a very positive way.

One of the problems which may arise from the use of the home office of one of the association members will result from this same "at home" feeling described above. The joint venture project cannot be treated as just another job in the office. It takes on a special identity which must be maintained throughout the life of the venture. Once established in the office, the project must be controlled under the separate rules established for the venture by the policy committee, even though these rules may differ from the office practice. Moreover, as a separate entity the project should be immune from the "raiding" of manpower which takes place in an office when another job of higher priority needs a sudden increase in manpower.

Another problem area may be the use of personnel from a different firm who are working in the home office. This arrangement can lead to conflicts of hours, salaries, benefits, procedures, and policies of many other areas. If the job is done in a home office, it is best that the staff come only from that office and, except in rare cases, that new staff be hired by that office rather than imported from other offices. Further discussion of this is found later in this chapter under the section entitled "Manpower."

The last area of possible conflict has to do with overhead costs. If the work is to be done in a particular office, mostly by personnel of that office, then the actual overhead cost of that office should be reimbursed to the office. While this may lead to criticism by other members of the venture that they could do it "cheaper in their own shops," nevertheless, if the decision is made to use the other fellow's office, the venture must pay the going rate for the services of that office. The other firms may help out by suggesting ways, from their own practices, by which costs could be saved, but this does not relieve them of paying the actual office overhead costs.

Locating in a Separate Office

Usually the project has to be quite sizable to select the option of establishing a separate office. However, if this decision is made, it affords the opportunity to engage premises which can substantially decrease the overhead costs of the project. It has been our experience that the establishment of a separate office has effected a great many economies, since the venture can exactly isolate those costs which directly refer to the venture; moreover, these costs are easily defined and measured. However, as mentioned before, the project must be of a size which can, for instance, support a full-time secretary or bookkeeper or office boy or other service personnel, since it is obvious that to support such people without having a full-time need for their services would be wasteful.

Wherever possible in the selection of the location of the separate office, it is advisable to find premises near the office of one of the participants, preferably nearest the firm which will do most of the work. In this way, management personnel can better service the venture, sharing the time with the home-office operation. This allows a more generous volunteering of the time of key personnel, while not burdening the project with an inordinate amount of supervisory time.

One of our most successful joint ventures resulted in part from the excellent selection of the location of the joint venture office. The partner who was selected to administer the venture, because of the demands of his own practice, could give only part time to the venture. We were lucky to find a vacant office space contiguous with this man's firm. In this way we could share both the man and the conference rooms of his office. Furthermore, it enabled us to have a quick source of additional personnel when the project demanded. On the other hand, the new space was remote enough (one had to go out into the public hall to travel from one office to the other) that there were no adverse effects from the proximity of spaces. Of importance to remember in the selection of a separate office is the following:

The space should be large enough to fulfill all the requirements of the project, including such support functions as general office, stock rooms, plan files, sample room, and conference rooms. However, if the new office is within easy walking distance of one of the home offices, then some of the support space may not be required. For this arrangement to work, the access must be direct and easy, since oftentimes many people will have to appear at a conference and the man hours wasted in bringing all these people to the meetings may more than offset the rental cost of the additional space. Another factor to consider carefully in the determination to use the space of one of the joint venture offices for the support services is the schedule and work load of the home office, since these spaces are vital to its function.

Another important consideration in the selection of the remote office location is the long-term availability of the space. How often have large-scale (especially governmental) projects taken a much longer period of time than anyone anticipated! Therefore, it is most important that the lease for any new facility be of sufficient length to cover the term of the contract as well as contain enough protection so that it can be extended beyond the original lease period. An example of the importance of this aspect occurred in the practice of our firm when our joint venture project had an extremely tight, almost inviolable time schedule of three years. Our client insisted that no additional time would be required or allowed by them. The only space we could find for the venture which met our criteria for location, size, and cost had a five-year lease period with it. Consequently, in our financial forecasts, we figured that we would have to take a loss in subleasing to others for the extra two-year period beyond the firm three-year term of the project. As is so often the case, circumstances well beyond the control of either the client or ourselves have delayed the project to the extent that we are now in our fifth year and are negotiating with the landlord to extend the lease even further.

In furnishing the remote office, it must be kept in mind that these premises, although temporary in nature, will serve as the working environment for a sizable number of people for many years. The efficiencies resulting from providing good working conditions, not only including the air conditioning and lighting but also the furniture and furnishings, will usually more than repay the additional initial costs.

The establishment of a separate office at the outset of a project requires high initial costs for furnishing. This usually means that the venturers are required to put up rather large sums of money at the start of the venture. To avoid this, many ventures begin their initial phase of work in the office of one of the member firms and then use the early payments from the client as a source of funds for leasing a separate office and purchasing equipment, etc. This procedure not only avoids high initial contributions from the partner firms, but also gives the venture a chance to establish itself before undertaking large financial commitments for separate facilities.

MANPOWER

The proper selection and control of personnel is the key to the successful completion of a joint venture project. Before discussing methods for achieving these goals, it might be worth while to analyze the qualities regarding manpower which make a joint venture project different from a project in the office of the individual practitioner.

Since in a joint venture only one project is usually involved, the flexibility and diversity which are usually found in the practice of the individual office are lacking. Thus all decisions must be made on the basis of the one job alone.

Several offices are involved in the joint venture; consequently, there can be several different sets of rules and regulations with respect to manpower. Any new rules which apply to the manpower of the joint venture must dovetail with the existing rules of the individual offices.

Most firms are competing for new projects during their normal operations, and most firms are constantly looking for competent personnel to produce their work. However, to maintain harmony between the various offices of a joint venture, competition for the manpower must be carefully avoided.

Since a joint venture project may involve the use of manpower from several offices working together, consideration must be given to the interaction between the individual and the rest of the personnel in the venture. If the assignment of a person to the work of the joint venture is made too attractive (whether in the home office or in a separate office), then jealousy might be created among those not "lucky" enough to be assigned to the venture's work. On the other hand, if the feeling is developed that working on this "foreign" project is akin to being exiled, the assignment takes on a negative status, and then unhappiness may also result. Therefore, a happy balance must be achieved so as to disrupt manpower as little as possible.

Competent personnel who have developed work under the system of the individual office must now be asked to develop work with someone else who may have a different set of criteria for performance. New methods, new experiences, new supervisory personnel. The challenge lies in limiting the negative effects on skilled and experienced people and turning their involvement into a positive learning experience.

These factors must be seriously considered and understood before manpower is assigned. Ideally, where the joint venture is produced in one of the home offices by the personnel already there, perhaps augmented by a few additional personnel to round out the staff requirements, there is a minimum of disruption. However, unhappy situations arise when the job requires either a large influx of new personnel into one of the home offices or the shifting of manpower from several offices to a separate joint venture office. It is here that a "mix" process, whose mechanics must be understood, takes place.

Establishing Office Standards

In the case where the work will be turned out in one of the home offices, we have found it best that the rules of that office apply to the work of the joint venture project. In this way there is little or no disruption of the established methods of operation. When a group of men from other offices or new men hired for the particular project arrive on the scene, they are indoctrinated into the ways of the office, which will also become procedure for the joint venture operation.

It is also best in this case that the supervisory personnel come from the same office, again to cause as little disruption as possible to the firm's modus operandi. This same method holds true when the work will be turned out in a succession of offices during different stages of the project. Each office in turn should, where possible, use a majority of its own staff and supervisory personnel, with a minimum of outside help. In this way conflict will be avoided. The problem, however, in this situation will be the necessity of maintaining a uniformity in all the work which will be submitted in the name of the joint venture. It is here that someone will have to establish the technical rules to which all must conform. In actual practice, this is easier than might be imagined at first blush. Since the work will be different in each stage (preliminary, working drawings, construction, etc.), exact uniformity is really not required. What should be insisted upon, however, is uniformity in the graphics, such as preprinted sheets and title blocks, a single address and point of contact, and other ways which signify to the owner that the joint venture is a single entity doing work on his project. It is important to maintain this same sensation of a single identity in the eyes of the members and personnel of the venture.

Where work will be accomplished in a separate office, the standards should be set by the venture, with the project manager having a strong voice in what rules will be established. Once these rules have been developed, they should be put down in writing and should remain the standard throughout the entire project.

Additional Manpower

Where additional personnel is required to staff the progress of the work in one of the joint venture home offices and where there are no additional men available from that office, it becomes necessary to decide whether the new men should be brought in from the other offices or whether they should be hired from the outside. Many factors must be weighed in making this decision. If there is a surplus of manpower in another venture firm's office which is close-by and has the type of personnel necessary for the efficient production of the work, then it seems best to call upon these men to do the job. However, an understanding must be developed with these men that this is a temporary job and that they, during their stay in the other office, will have to abide by the rules and practices of that office. Another important feature to remember is that the lending office must pledge to keep the men at the new office for the time period agreed upon, so as not to disrupt the operation of the joint venture's work. This agreement must be kept, despite the fact that the originating office may suddenly become busy and require the men to return to the home office.

If, however, there is no extra manpower at any of the other offices or, by reason of remote location, the wrong type of personnel is available, then the home office must go out and hire the necessary men. In order to avoid the stigma of the office's being labeled a "hire and fire" office, these men might be assigned to the payroll of several offices, despite the fact that they might be working in only one of the offices.

This type of operation led to an interesting experience. We had on our payroll several men who had never reported to our office but were working in the office of one of our joint venture partners. The joint venture work slowed down, and several of the men on our payroll were dismissed. One of them then applied for a job in our home office. Despite the fact that he had been on our payroll for several years, we had to call our joint venturer to find out how good he was!

Incidentally, we have always made it a practice that any employment agency fees which must be paid to obtain new personnel for the venture would be reimbursed to the firm hiring the man.

One thing which must be avoided at all costs is the consideration of the joint venture as the "dumping ground" for unskilled or superfluous personnel. The venture must be allowed to operate as efficiently as your own practice and in order to do so requires the cooperation of each partner to supply the best men available, whether from in-house staff or elsewhere. As a standard for maintaining high-quality manpower, it is usually best to allow the project manager to determine the manpower needs and the acceptability of the men supplied to the project by the various offices. His judgment should become the unquestioned authority in the selection and maintenance of the personnel levels. Furthermore, it is incumbent on all the joint venture firms to respond on a timely basis to his call for additional manpower. We have always found it wise, when there is not sufficient staff available from the various offices and additional men must be employed, to have the project manager do the soliciting and interviewing, since he alone is in the best position to determine what type of man is necessary for the good of the whole operation. The new man is then assigned to the payroll of one of the participating firms.

Employee Benefits   When the project is produced in one of the joint venture offices, it is usual that the job benefits granted the joint venture's employees would be the same as that practiced by the office in which the work is done. The costs of these benefits would, of course, be reimbursed to the office paying them, on the basis of a percentage of payroll cost or by another agreed-upon method.

Where, however, a separate office is established, the type and amount of benefits are something to be carefully considered. The problem arises from the fact that the various employees in the joint office are actually on the payroll of the different offices, while all working together in the same office. Some, therefore, will be having their hospitalization insurance fully paid by the home office, while others might pay their own. In another instance, the kind and number of holidays might vary from office to office. This is especially true of offices in different parts of the country. How, then, is harmony established among the men and conflict avoided?

We have found the best way to prevent major problems is to separate the various categories of employee benefits and to treat them individually. In this way, order and understanding are established.

Working Hours   No matter what the working hours of the individual offices, the schedule of hours established in the office in which the work is done determines the working hours for the venture. If a separate office is established, a schedule is decided upon for the new office, and this schedule prevails.

Complication can arise where one office is used to working 40 hours, while another only 35 or 37½ hours. The problem is to combine these different schedules into an efficient and happy office. There is especially a problem if the men are now being compensated on a weekly rate. Who would want to work for 40 hours for the same pay he now receives for working 35 hours? The solution which we have employed to best advantage is to follow this procedure, once the hourly schedule has been established. Anyone who now would be working more hours than he used to will have his pay raised in direct ratio to cover the additional hours; anyone now required to work fewer hours will continue to receive the same pay. In this way, nobody loses and everyone wins.

Holidays   Whenever the venture is carried out at one of the home offices, the holiday schedule for that office prevails. In a new office for the joint venture, a new schedule is established, and all employees of the office are required to adhere to the schedule. Usually, for the separate office the tendency is to adopt the most liberal holiday policy of the various members. Again, no one loses.

Morale   It is important for the various offices of a joint venture to understand some of the stresses, unique to a joint venture operation, which affect the men of an office when they are required to report to a separate or another joint venture office. Unfortunately, the impression is often gained that the person selected is being sent away because he has not measured up to the standards of the home office. The reverse impression must be developed; he must be made to feel that this is a special assignment, reserved only for the *most* qualified. Aspects supporting this contention include the fact that the joint venture project is a very large and complicated one requiring the use of only the most skilled manpower. Moreover, the man's value is confirmed by the fact that each joint venture partner owes a particular allegiance to the other members of the venture whom they do not want to let down by supplying other than the best possible personnel.

Another worry that frequently arises regarding the men assigned to the remote office is that he will lose seniority or other privileges while away. Reassurance in this case takes the form of frequent contact maintained between the employee and his office. Whenever possible, a partner should stop by to "visit" whenever he is around for a meeting or review. Other ways include keeping in frequent telephone contact and allowing the employee the opportunity to visit the home office occasionally. In addition, our office, at a time when we had several remote joint ventures being developed simultaneously, starting publishing an office newsletter, the *Grad-About,* which was circulated to all the various offices. It is important, too, to invite these men back to the home office for the company picnic, the Christmas party, and other functions. The key theme to remember is that while the employee is remote, he still considers himself an employee of the firm from which he came. This is his home and his security.

Miscellaneous Items   Other areas related to manpower which should be considered by the home office include such things as relocation expenses. When a key person is forced to make a major move in order to service a joint venture, the costs of relocation should be borne by the joint venture rather than by the individual office from which the man came. In some instances, where a large geographical distance exists between a man's home office and the place in which he would be expected to serve the joint venture, other equalizing adjustments may have to be made. For instance, if there is a major difference in the cost of living, adjustments must be made to the scheme of compensation so that the man feels he is being equally treated. Because of these complications, we have found it best to confine any major relocations to a few personnel only. Of course, where operations in foreign countries are part of the joint venture development, the means and methods of providing equitable compensation are very important factors in determining the man's happiness and efficiency. These considerations include tax advice, relocation of family, even the cost of foreign-language lessons, when necessary for the carrying out of the man's job.

The different home office policies regarding employee benefits such as hospitalization, pensions, profit sharing plans, etc., are usually continued without change for their employees furnished to the joint venture office.

COMPLETING THE PROJECT

In reality, as far as its technical aspects, there is very little difference in the development of a joint venture project compared to one turned out in a large office. The client has certain requirements, and the professionals respond to these demands. The only difference, therefore, is in the interrelationship of the various individuals from separate offices. What is produced should be nearly the same as that put out by one office. In fact, that is the goal: to have the project appear as if it were developed by a single firm. However, there are certain areas of the operation which should receive special attention to avoid having confusion arise from lack of coordination.

Communication

This aspect of the project is an especially serious one. When one realizes how difficult real communication is even in a single office, what then of the several offices which comprise the association? Here the problem becomes even more critical.

Every party to the joint venture has a right to know exactly what is going on throughout the project. Systems must be devised to answer this need. One person should be assigned the responsibility of communication; usually, this is the project manager. All minutes of meetings as well as important correspondence must be distributed to all the parties involved. All decisions must be reviewed with the policy committee. We have found it best to err on the side of overdoing the amount of information disseminated, since each party receiving this information has a right to ignore the material or dispose of it in the way he sees best.

In addition to technical information, there is also the financial and business data. Here again, one party, usually the person appointed as business manager, is given the responsibility for forwarding important information to all parties.

We have often found it of value to request opinion responses from the recipient firms. In this way one can really take advantage of the inherent value of a venture, the composite of many firms with a broad range of expertise.

Correspondence which is sent to the client will usually originate from the project manager. However, any letters which have legal or financial importance should be signed by an officer of each participating firm. In addition to lending more importance to the letter, it also serves to protect the individual parties of the venture and represents to the client that the subject of the letter was the product of the entire venture.

Uniformity of Effort

One of the aspects which makes the venture different from the work developed by the single firm is the problem that various types of office standards may creep into the work as a result of the different offices participating in the effort. Such items as standard symbols and representations will usually vary with the individual offices participating in the work. At the beginning of the project, new standards which represent the work of the new "office," the joint venture, must be established and must be followed without deviation. Here, again, pride must be assuaged, since each office usually thinks that its methods are far superior to those of other offices. As usual, any conflict that arises should be cleared by the policy committee, and its decisions should be strictly enforced. In many government and large corporate projects, the client is the party who dictates much of the standard criteria used in the project, thus avoiding the conflict of various standards. No matter, however, what the source of the standards, their uniform use throughout the project is the important concern.

This rule is especially hard to follow when the work is produced in several offices. In this case, despite the fact that the adopted standards may differ from the norm of the remainder of the office, they must be enforced for the work of the joint venture. One party, usually the project manager, should be given the responsibility to review and control this aspect. Of course, when the work will be produced in the office of one of the venturers, the standards of that office should be adopted, unless there is good reason for changing them. Again, here is one of the areas in which the individual firms may learn from one another's practice. A review of the way in which the individual firms operate can be very instructive to the other firms, who may consequently adopt new methods after observing those of another firm.

The object of the entire effort is the production of the best technical product with the minimum of effort and disruption of the practice of the individual joint venturer's offices. The product must always appear the result of a unified effort.

CHAPTER TEN

Administering the Effort

In addition to the technical effort required to turn out the work, there are many administrative functions which must take place during the course of the joint venture project. The exercise of these administrative controls will in great measure determine the financial success of the project. In addition, the administrative effort helps determine how the individual venturers "feel" about the association. This in turn affects greatly the interrelationship of the individual partners in the common effort. For example, if a partner feels that the venture is a "losing proposition," he may not supply his best men to the effort, opting to keep them for the more rewarding projects of his private practice. Unfortunately, this in turn will probably cause the joint venture project to suffer even more, creating a feeling of even greater unhappiness among the partners. Consequently it may continue to disintegrate. Proper controls are necessary to avoid these problems.

FINANCIAL CONTROL

As in any other business undertaking, the financial aspects are of major importance. With only a few exceptions the control of this area is similar to the parallel function in the individual office. Basically, the important steps are the actual establishment of procedures and their implementation. As with most everything else, the creation of control must all start with an agreement to put someone in charge and a definition of methods to control the finances.

The Business Manager

Just as the technical effort must receive the right kind of leadership, so must the financial aspects be run by someone knowledgeable. We have found it of value in our joint ventures to name one individual as the business manager to control the financial affairs of the association. Usually this is a partner of one of the firms who has the same type of responsibility in his own practice. He will be aided by a staff of people selected for the particular needs of the project. These people are usually on the business manager's own staff, and unless the joint venture is of extremely large magnitude, they will supply part-time effort to the venture in addition to fulfilling their own home-office responsibilities.

In the joint venture chain of command, the business manager is responsible to the policy committee. His function is to control all business affairs of the venture and to keep all members aware of these aspects. Necessarily, the actual administrative functions of the business manager will vary greatly with the kind and extent of the project. We will attempt here to describe some of the more usual financial activities which may occur during the life of the venture.

The Administrative File

The repository of all administrative items of correspondence as well as reports and other information bearing on the administrative aspects of the venture will be kept by the business manager. Each individual home office will contain its own file, complete to the degree they deem necessary. Important, however, is the fact that the complete file will be kept in one location. In many instances, this location is remote from the main technical file. This should pose no problem unless poor communication is established.

Accounting Systems and Standard Forms

The business manager will determine the type of forms which will be used in the exercise of the management of the venture. Usually, he will make a presentation to the policy committee at the start of the project, explaining the methods he has chosen to use on behalf of the venture. At this time systems may be discussed and changed to better suit the project. Once these are agreed upon, it is expected that they will be executed throughout the remainder of the venture.

The systems established at this time usually include the methods of how monies will be deposited when received, how payments will be dispensed to the various partners for work supplied to the venture, how consultants will be paid, and how profits will be distributed. They also include a discussion of tax matters and a decision of which reports at what frequency will be sent out to the venture members.

The selection of an accountant should be made at the inception of the project. He will aid in setting up the bookkeeping systems and will provide advice to the business manager and the policy committee on financial matters. Usually it is best that the accounting firm chosen be located near the office of the business manager so that there is ease of access. Because of the peculiar nature of some aspects of the joint venture organization, it is wisest to choose an accountant who has had prior experience with this type of operation.

Banking

In most instances, because payment comes only after work is accomplished, the joint venture members will have to make an initial payment to finance the joint venture at the start of the project. The amount of this payment is usually specified in the joint venture agreement, and it usually is proportional to the equity position each partner has in the venture. This money is used in the establishment of a joint venture checking account. The number of signatures required on the check will vary with the venture. Factors such as the proximity to each other, previous joint experience of this type, and the size of the undertaking will all play a part in this determination. Usually, where it is possible without causing too much delay or inefficiency, it is best that representatives of at least two firms be required to sign all checks. In this way, not only is there a built-in safeguard, but also a broader degree of participation can take place. There has been some criticism of this method. Some feel that it is inefficient in that it takes too long to operate. Others state that it often puts the cosigner in a position in which he is approving a payment without knowing the full reasons of its issuance, since all details are impossible to transmit. Despite these criticisms, however, we have found it best to involve more than one signer in the check-writing procedure.

A method of control found of value where the dual-signature method is impractical is the dual bank account system. When enough money is received, another account is opened, possibly in a savings bank, in addition to the checking account. All payments received are deposited in this other account which requires two signatures to withdraw funds. The operation of the checking account in this system requires only one signature. In this way a system of control of the larger amounts of money is possible, without unnecessarily delaying the operation of the business of the venture. No matter what method is employed, it is of prime importance that an organized system for the dissemination of business information be established to keep all partners informed of the progress of the finances of the project. Further, the partnership should have the flexibility to change any system that proves unworkable, through a vote of the policy committee, usually upon request of the business manager.

Distributing Financial Information

A good system of distribution of financial information is the cornerstone of a successful venture. Each partner firm is curious to know what is happening to the economic position of the project. Generally, statements are distributed monthly to the members of the policy committee, which show the cash position of the venture up to the moment. A statement on a cash and/or accrual basis will be prepared quarterly by the accountant and circulated to all members. This statement will indicate the overall profit-loss picture and record the interest of each of the parties in the venture.

In ventures where each party responsible for a portion of the work receives the profits from this portion, other systems of distribution of financial information are possible. With rare exception, however, the greater the distribution of the financial knowledge, the less likely the possibility of friction among the partners regarding financial affairs. Disclosure should be on a need-to-know basis, with as much information as possible accurately developed and widely distributed.

We have also found it good policy to send to all partner firms copies of major billings made to the client. In this way they are kept current with all the receivables and receive a good guide to the progress of the work as it is being developed. Further, where the individual firms have contacts with the same client, they may aid in the collection of the funds due the joint venture.

Since the income of the joint venture will affect the tax picture of the various participating firms, it becomes important that the financial information be made available to the members of the venture on a timely basis, so that each firm can properly plan its own financial position. Based on this requirement, it is usually helpful for the venture accountant to make a projection early in December of the probable financial status of the venture, including the year-end income and the distributive share to the parties involved. This provision allows enough time for the partners to examine their own financial situations as well as to help in adjusting the finances of the venture to the benefit of the majority of the parties. A problem may arise when one of the partner firms would prefer to have as little income as possible for the joint venture during that particular year, because of a large projected income from its own practice; on the other hand, the other partner who has had a poor year would not mind paying taxes on the income from the joint venture for the year. This conflict must be resolved between the parties, with the help of their own accountants if necessary. Each party must report his distributive share of income shown on the tax form for the venture. This reported income has nothing to do with the actual cash distributions among the partner firms; the latter depends upon the cash flow of the venture.

Charting the Progress of the Project

Each office in a joint venture has established control methods within its own practice. These systems, particularly for the control of cost and time, may vary from simple word-of-mouth exchanges of progress reports to elaborate, computerized reporting systems. Similarly, the systems developed for the venture will vary with the participants and the scope of the project. However, what must be stressed here is the need for a valid reporting system so that the members of the venture will be kept continually informed of the progress of the work. This is especially critical where the members of the venture are in distant cities and therefore cannot easily determine the degree of progress of the work from their own observations. In our experience, controls must be exercised over the two important areas of *budgeting* the project and *scheduling* the project.

Budgeting the Project

Of interest to all members of the venture is how well the job is succeeding in earning the potential profit. The first step, therefore, is to establish the budget, a goal against which the financial progress will be measured. While the actual method of establishing the budget may vary, setting a realistic target is the aim. Figure 10-1 shows a typical budget form.

In this way, the number of dollars required to complete each phase of the project is established. This calculation is periodically compared to the actual amount of money expended. Every two weeks the project manager estimates the percentage of completion of the current phase of the project. The actual amount of dollars spent is then compared to the amount of dollars that was anticipated to be spent to accomplish the estimated percentage of completion. A report is then issued to the members of the venture, showing the status of the project in terms of dollars earned compared to dollars spent. A typical budget report is the form in Figure 10-2.

JOINT VENTURE PROJECT BUDGET

PROJECT No. ....

....

BUDGET No. ....

DATE ....

1. ESTIMATED FEE:

    BASIC: % x   =

    EXTRAS: =

                                        ....

                                                      $ .... (100%)

2. FEES TO CONSULTANTS:

    STRUCTURAL   % x   =

    MECH. & ELECT.   % x   =

    KITCHEN   % x   =

    LANDSCAPE   % x   =

    ESTIMATOR   =

    OTHER   =

                                        ....

                                                      .... (%)

3. AVAILABLE TO J.V. (1–2)   ....

4. ESTIMATED PROFIT   =   (%)

5. ESTIMATED DIRECT EXPENSES =   (%)

                                        ....

                                                      ....

6. AVAILABLE FOR OH & DIRECT PAYROLL (3–5)   ....

7. ALLOWANCE FOR OVERHEAD   .... (%)

8. AVAILABLE FOR DIRECT PAYROLL (6–7)   .... (%)

DIRECT PAYROLL BREAKDOWN

SCHEMATIC DESIGN   .... % $ ....

DESIGN DEVELOPMENT   .... %   ....

CONSTR. DOCUMENTS   .... %   ....

CONSTRUCTION ADMIN.   .... %   ....

                                        100%   ....

FIG. 10-1

In this instance, as in so many other cases, the decision of which form to use often allows the various members of the venture to study methods used by the other firms. They may then possibly alter their own forms or adopt another firm's form if it appears more satisfactory.

JOINT VENTURE BUDGET REPORT

PROJECT No. ....

....

REPORT No. ....

DATE ....

1 PHASE	2 PAYROLL BUDGET	3 % COMP	4 BUDGET SPENT	5 ACTUAL SPENT	6 4 − 5	7 6 + OH
SCHEMATIC						
DESIGN DEV.						
CONST. DOC.						
CONSTRUCTION						
TOTALS						

$$\frac{\text{COL. 4}}{\text{COL. 2}}$$

FIG. 10-2

Scheduling the Project

As in so many activities, time is money and, as such, must be carefully controlled in order to realize a successful project. Quite often the time schedule becomes an essential condition of the contract, and the control of time then becomes a prime factor in the development of the work.

The time scheduling for a joint venture project should vary little from the scheduling activities taking place in the various offices of the venture. In addition to the target dates appearing on the schedule, it is often useful to list the important activities as well as the party responsible for fulfilling the required task. This list should include joint venture members, the consultants, and the client. All share responsibility for some part of the work.

Our firm has found it valuable to use a modified Critical Path Method (CPM) chart as an excellent method in scheduling the work. We try carefully to prethink the project, listing the task and designating the party who must accomplish each part of the work. Thus the individual joint venturers, the owner, and all others involved have before them both the targets to shoot for and the member who is responsible for the shooting! It is important that the owner know what his responsibilities are. Mainly, he must furnish information at the start of a project and grant approvals on a timely basis as the work is developed. This schedule must be updated periodically so that the status of the project is always current. Copies of the status reports are sent to the owner and the venture members and are reported upon at the policy committee meetings.

Quite often the client will have a system of time-schedule reporting which he has developed and insists upon using. In this case, the client's standard format will be used; when the report is prepared for the owners, copies of it will be sent to the venture firms.

INSURANCE PROGRAM

As far as insurance is concerned, a joint venture requires the same type of insurance coverage as any private firm. If a separate office is opened, separate policies should be taken out which protect the joint venture the same way as they would a private individual firm.

Each firm participating in the joint venture should continue to maintain its own individual insurance coverage, including Workmen's Compensation; bodily injury, including personal injury, sickness or disease and/or death of any of its employees or others; and property damage insurance. This requirement for the individual firm's insurance is sometimes recorded in the joint venture agreement.

Special insurance which should be considered for the architectural and/or engineering venture is *professional liability insurance.* Joint ventures can no longer benefit from the individual "errors and omissions" coverage under the separate firms' policies. The venture must secure its own coverage.

This is done through direct application by the venture to the agency selling the insurance. Usually, the information requested by the company includes the name of the joint venture, the project, the estimated construction value, the estimated time for design and construction, the amount of coverage, and the deductible amount. Based upon this information, the agency will submit an estimate of the premium. A sample joint venture insurance estimate form, received from Victor O. Schinnerer and Company, Inc., of Washington, D.C., is shown in Figure 10-3.

The professional liability insurance must remain in force after the completion of the project and throughout the period not covered by the applicable state statute of limitations. Note that the joint venture estimate form allows for the purchase of coverage for a twelve-year discovery period. Consult with your attorney and insurance man for advice as to length and type of extended coverage.

Another form of insurance which might be taken out by the joint venture is fidelity bond coverage for all persons who are directly involved in the handling of money or other valuables for the venture.

Advice from an experienced insurance agent can be helpful in setting up the entire joint venture insurance program. His function in reviewing the adequacy of the coverage of the various firms and in recommending joint coverage can supply the unbiased advice which is often quite essential.

THE PUBLIC RELATIONS PROGRAM

As in any going practice, the public relations program must be established and carried through. In a joint venture, this is one aspect which must receive special attention. The need for this accentuation results from the fact that we are dealing with several firms, some of whom are normally in competition with each other. They would resent deeply any unfair advantage which one firm may enjoy over the others in the matter of the public image put forth during the course of the venture. The key word in the establishment of publicity in the venture is fairness and equality among all the members. Adherence to this policy must be strict in order to avoid unhappiness and controversy.

Date: November 13, 1970

JOINT VENTURE ESTIMATES

Re: Associated Shopping Center Architects

Project: Shopping Center Plaza

Estimated Construction Value: $3,000,000.

Estimated Time for Design and Construction: 3 years

Limit of liability	Deductible and loss contribution		Project premium including 12-year discovery	To eliminate deductible on bodily injury (or death) only claims	To include coverage for libel, slander, defamation of character
	Minimum	Maximum			
$1,000,000.	$5,000.	$10,000.	$3,334.	$70.	$100.

Premiums for joint venture coverage are based on the total construction value of the project, regardless of the length of time required for design and construction. These quotations are estimates of premiums based on the estimated construction values which you have given us, and the current rates. The final premium would be subject to adjustment based on the final construction cost and any changes in rates during the life of the project.

These quotations include coverage for professional errors, omissions or negligent acts committed in connection with the project, provided claim is made against the insured within 12 years of the completion of the project.

Coverage during the design and construction period will be provided by annual policies. At the expiration of the annual policy in force at the completion of the project that policy will be endorsed to provide the 12-year discovery period from that date.

The premium for each annual policy may be determined by dividing the project premium quoted above by the number of years required for design and construction.

To effect coverage, simply send us your check for the annual premium and indicate the coverage desired.

FIG. 10-3

In the case of a large venture, an individual or firm may be given the responsibility to develop the public relations program and carry it through. As in any undertaking of this kind, the program is only as good as the time and effort which members of the joint venture can devote to it. It is best to have the selected individual deal directly with the policy committee in establishing both the objectives and the program necessary to achieve these goals. Once this agreement has been reached, the man can then work with the individuals in the firm who are in the best position to help. Technical information should be gotten from the project manager, while the business-related items should be established with the business manager. All releases should be cleared by the members of the policy committee.

It is important that all releases bear the name of all joint venture members. Any personal appearances should, wherever possible, have partners from all participating firms present. All photographs should have all members included.

It is possible, however, to emphasize one firm in special situations without losing the equality which is so important. For instance, if the various firms are located in different cities, a release which emphasizes the local firm could be developed and distributed to the different cities. So, the headlines in the *Newark News* and *New Orleans Times Picayune* might both read, "Local Architect Designs Largest Building in Washington," but each paper would be featuring a different architect. Both stories, however, will mention that the local architect is part of a joint venture group of architects working together on the project. This same situation applies to the venture of several professions. In this case, the engineer could be featured in the engineering journal for the imaginative solutions which he developed in the project, while the architect may similarly be covered in the architectural journal for his handsome design. Again, however, it is important to establish the fact that each firm was working as part of a joint venture whose responsibility was the development of the entire project.

With the aid of a trained and talented public relations person, the identity of the joint venture may be established as not just a temporary combination of firms, but as a solid separate entity. In this instance, establishing a separate name of a unique identity through a logo design could be quite helpful in creating this separate and distinct image. The promulgation of this new identity becomes especially important when the joint venture members have decided that they like to work together and have determined that they want to go out and obtain more work for the association of firms.

For the smaller project, the establishment of the public relations program may not seem as important. However, a different judgment may be rendered when it is realized that not only does the venture benefit from publicity, but the individual firms and clients as well. In the case of the smaller project, the duties of developing the publicity may be handled by a member of one of the participating firms; however, no matter by whom it is handled, the basic requirement for equality must remain the keyword.

MAINTAINING CONTINUITY

It is especially important in the joint venture project that continuity with the client be established early and be maintained throughout the project. As described earlier in the book, the owner enters the relationship with trepidation, regarding what he sees as the likelihood of poor communication and inefficient management on the part of this temporary group of professional firms he has hired to accomplish his work. So it is important to reassure him and at the same time to help your association by both establishing a firm chain of command and continuing the same throughout the project. Most often, however, this communication system seems to fall down during the later stages of the work. In projects which result in a construction stage, there is often a tendency to lessen the effort expended, especially by the principals of the project. While this is true of most individual practices, it seems even more evident in a joint venture project. The reasons are evident enough. By the construction stage of the work, the project has gone through many months and many events. The glamorous, creative phases have been completed and the "challenges" posed by the checking of shop drawings and contractors' payment requisitions are not very exciting to the partners. But they still have to be done. Furthermore, many a repeat job has been lost because the client feels neglected, or even abandoned, by the venture partners during the construction period. So it is important in the joint venture operation, as well as in any other project, that the principals maintain the same high level of communication and effort during this phase of the work.

Actually, a joint venture is in a better position to service this phase of the work since it has many more principals available than the usual single firm. Some effective ways to maintain the image of partners' interest during this stage include:

Holding the policy committee meetings at the site. This gives the partners a chance to see the project and the owner a chance to see the partners.

Developing a site-visitation schedule for the principals in which each in turn shows up at the site and meets the client. Of course, the partner must be "clued in" by the project manager before his appearance so that he will be knowledgeable about the progress and problems of the project.

Telephone contact by principals with the client to discuss the project.

Meanwhile, the venture's effort proceeds. Often, because of the limited requirement for manpower during the construction stage, the separate joint venture office is closed up, and work continues in one of the offices or in a field office. The project manager continues to service the project with such staff as he requires. Periodic policy committee meetings should be held to keep all parties informed of what is currently happening. Important reports and correspondence must continue to be disseminated to all interested parties. Enthusiasm for the project is renewed through the circulation of progress photographs and visits to the site.

There is still nothing to equal the thrill of seeing a building grow from the drawings you have developed.

CHAPTER ELEVEN

Minimizing the Negative

As is true in practically every activity involving a group of human beings, there are bound to be certain undesirable aspects which become apparent as the association develops. The success of the undertaking usually depends upon the ability of those involved to emphasize the positive aspects while minimizing the less desirable qualities. A joint venture is no different.

We all recognize that no two people are alike. Different ages, backgrounds, training, motivation, and personalities and the many other human traits lead each of us to think and feel differently about each circumstance. These inherent differences lead to misunderstanding and possible dispute. To assure a smooth-flowing, happy project, the major areas of potential problems should be understood and controlled. The common theme throughout this book is that the key to success lies in the prior understanding of problems to be encountered and written agreement of how they are to be solved.

In the joint venture of design professionals, there are two

major areas of potential problems which must be understood and controlled. They both concern basic human qualities and, as such, will vary greatly among different people, as a function of an individual's own personal traits. These problems are cited in this book as a warning that they can pose a serious threat to the well-being of the venture; therefore, they must be taken into consideration at the early stages of the venture, and methods must be devised to avoid the negative results which may be forthcoming.

THE EGO FACTOR

Design professionals are creative people. As such, they usually possess a strong belief in the strength of their own ideas. Since the solutions to a particular design problem may be many and varied, there seems to be a tendency by creative individuals to reinforce their own solutions by rejecting those of others. As a result, the ideas expressed by others seem to take a secondary role in the eyes of the egotist. This is certainly a fine and almost necessary trait for the individual design practitioner to possess, since it gives him the strength of his own convictions in the selling of his ideas or designs. In many instances the client is looking for this quality of sureness to convince him about a subject he usually knows very little about. He relies upon the "expert."

The problem arises, however, when several professionals, each individually possessed of excellent design ability, are given the collective responsibility of designing a project together. Each, normally master of his own bailiwick, with proved success behind him, must now share the driver's seat with others.

From research around the country, it has been demonstrated that the ego problem can be the largest source of headache to the smooth operation of a joint venture. It also affects the client, since he is the one who ultimately must pay for the error, delay, and unhappiness which may spring forth from this type of problem. The best demonstration of the seriousness of the problems which may result from this type of ego conflict in joint ventures comes from the recitation of a few actual cases.

Several architects were given the project to design a major government office building. Each architect in his own right fancied himself an excellent designer. They had a right to these feelings, since they were all highly successful practitioners. In fact, these architects were all practicing in the same city and were normally competitors for the largest jobs. They had been forcibly married by the government agency because of the tremendous size of the project. Only through the combination of these firms could the government assure itself that the project would receive sufficient manpower and expertise.

The project began with the partners of the three firms forming a policy and operating committee. One of their first decisions was to not set up a separate office until after the preliminary drawings were accomplished. Furthermore, to develop the schematic design, the committee decided to have an in-house design competition among the three offices. The idea was that each office would submit a design to the committee which would, in turn, choose the design that would be submitted to the client and developed further. Each office worked hard on its design submittal; in fact, the partners of each firm supervised and participated deeply in the development of the firm's submittal to the "competition." The fact that this project was of tremendous scope and unique quality spurred each office to produce a real winner. The judgment was held. Each office in turn presented its entry to the partner's committee. A secret vote was taken. Each entry received one vote. A three-way tie! Another vote was taken; again it was a dead heat. A discussion was then held about the merits of each design. The partner from the office whose design was being discussed rose to defend *his* design against the criticism of the other offices. The meeting became extremely heated without reaching any agreement. It was finally decided, after several meetings in which attempts were made to find a resolution of this dilemma, that the best thing to do was expose all designs to the client and let him decide which one he felt was best. Imagine the embarrassment of the client when he was confronted with this type of decision! Certainly the image of the joint venture suffered as a result, as did the architecture, for the nonarchitect client chose parts of one design added to parts of the other two presentations.

In another case, two partners' inability to agree resulted in a similar competition in front of the client. No decision was made before lunchtime, although each principal had personally presented his firm's design. Because of a prior arrangement, while one of the parties had a luncheon appointment elsewhere, the other ate with the client. After the lunch hour, when all parties had reassembled, the client accepted the design of the joint venture member who had coincidentally had lunch with him. The other party never forgave his associate for "unduly influencing" the client during the luncheon. This allegation was denied, of course, by the successful party. No matter what the actual circumstances, the rift created by this decision set the stage for bad feelings and mistrust throughout the remainder of the project, and all parties suffered, including the client.

While the architectural profession may appear to suffer more from this ego syndrome than others, similar occurrences are easy to visualize among other design professionals, or among designers and builders, etc. Imagine the conflict between the architect and the contractor in a joint venture in which design and building are the main ingredients. Both the parties have a stake in the financial outcome of the project, and, for example, the architect insists upon a particular costly detail which he considers a vital ingredient for the aesthetic quality of a project. The builder has solved this detail many times previously in a much less costly way, with results which he believes are aesthetically pleasing enough to justify the resultant saving in cost. How are these personal judgments to be resolved without controversy? Remember, these problems are very rarely a matter of right or wrong, but rather individual opinions about what should be.

This question of ego becomes a matter which must be resolved before it gets a chance to become a major hindrance to the successful completion of a project. To avoid problems in this area, there are several basic steps which may be taken. However, before reviewing these procedures, it must be noted that, as in any complex human relationship, there is not one set answer which will solve all problems. An understanding of the personalities of the individuals involved, as well as the scope of the problem, will usually determine the best solution available. It is really no different from solving the problems in any partnership. One advantage of a joint venture, in this respect, is that it is a *temporary* partnership that will dissolve by itself after the project is finished. Thus, patience is often the best solution to controversy.

Generally, we have found that the major method of offsetting the ego problem, as well as every other potential problem which may beset a joint venture, is the early and exact definition, in as fine detail as possible, of the individual responsibilities of the various parties involved. Here again, as it is voiced throughout this book, knowledge is the sword to cut through the problem and provide the solution. In many ventures, to avoid the potential conflict of egos involved in the design phases of a project, at the outset the design responsibility is given *in writing* to one of the parties. His job is clearly to get the design done, usually subject to the approval of the policy committee. In many instances, the designation of who will have the design responsibility may not be a matter for the joint venture parties to decide, but rather it may be dictated by the client; in this event, it is so stated in the agreement between owner and joint venture. To enforce this responsibility, many times the joint venture agreement among the parties will contain the stipulation that the ultimate decisions on any design element will repose in one principal's or one firm's hands, without right by the other parties to appeal. Pretty stiff language, but very effective as a tool to control the ego problem.

After having been exposed to many problems which result from the conflict among several design professionals in joint venture, the General Services Administration has often chosen the path of designating one firm to serve as the design leader of a joint venture. GSA has found that this is the most effective way to avoid problems similar to those described above. By the same token, there are many firms that would not form a joint venture unless they could control the design.

There are, however, problems associated with this method of designating the design leader. First, of course, there remains the now slightly tarnished egos of the other members of the team who were not chosen. Because in their own firms they still retain this leadership, this is a hard pill to swallow.

However, with patience and understanding this problem can usually be overcome. The other related problems are more difficult to resolve, since they have to do with the work to be performed by the other partners. These points are best illustrated by examples.

Assume that one member of a team has been given the design responsibility for a project, while the other member will produce the working drawings and specifications. Both have signed a contract which contains a clause that the joint venture must produce a project within a strict budget amount. If the construction bids received substantially exceed this amount, the agreement states that the contract documents must be revised, at the venture's own expense, to bring the price within the budget. The design partner creates the design which he feels is within the budget. The production partner protests that it looks too expensive, but he is overruled by the design partner. The contract documents are produced, are bid, and then have to be redrawn by reason of excessive cost. If the financial arrangement is such that each partner receives the profit for the part of the work he develops, the production partner is in a terrible plight. However, if both share the profits or losses from the entire job, then they may both suffer.

Other instances occur when there is a tight time schedule involved for the entire project. Suppose the design partner is slow, leaving little time for the production partner to produce the contract documents. The following is an example of this type of problem. Firm A was told by the client that Firm B, located in another city, was to be responsible for the design, while Firm A had the responsibility for the production of contract documents and the supervision of construction. The design office designated by the owner was the firm of a famous architect and was staffed primarily by students and recent graduates. Compounding the problem in this instance was the decision that each phase would be produced in the individual offices of the different participants. The designs produced were imaginative but almost impossible to detail. Moreover, few valid detail drawings were forthcoming from the design office both because the students were unavailable to perform the work and because those who did had no experience in the detailing of buildings. Getting the required drawings became increasingly more difficult, and those that were received were impossible. Add to this mixture an impossible schedule and a firm low budget, and the project looked for a while like sure disaster. Conferences between parties resolved nothing. The final answer was to take the entire project into the production office and to change the design as necessary to assure production of the work on time and within the budget, while trying to change the design as little as possible. It was a difficult project for everyone, including the owner.

Again, it must be stated that this type of problem should not be regarded as an architect's problem alone. For instance, if an architect and an engineer form a joint venture, both being collectively responsible for redesign costs, and if one overdesigns his phase of the work, they both suffer the costly consequences. So in effect each party must be aware of his responsibility to the other and keep this as the highest priority of the project.

Examples of the consequences of ego-conflict are included here to provide warning signals to new joint venturers. Perhaps if they are made aware of the existence of these problems, they will be better able to cope with them and to find viable solutions.

Another tested solution which we have found helpful in solving the designer's ego problem is through the establishment of a "design team" to produce the design of a project. In this method, each office designates one lead designer to work with the others to establish the basic design of the complex. Together they determine the main design vocabulary and direction, and they establish a method of accomplishment. Periodically, they display their progress to the policy committee for a critique. In this way, all participate. If the project is very large, the team may decide, once the basic direction is established, to give out parts of the design to individual members of the team, all of whom would be subject to the team's control of uniformity of design and concept. Often, the team will elect a leader both to maintain this control and to increase the efficiency of operation.

Another area where the excess desire for individual recognition may cause problems is in the presentations to client and public. When one party thrusts himself forward as representing the joint venture, he becomes identified with the entire project as if it were his own. This tends to put the other parties in the background, and they usually do not like this. Again, it takes a carefully defined effort to control this aspect. Sometimes, procedures to prevent conflict are included in the joint venture agreement. The best method to employ in making presentations to the client is to have all parties present at the meeting and to divide the responsibilities among them. In this way, all share in the spotlight. The public relations aspect must also be carefully planned for sharing as described in Chapter 10.

FINANCIAL JEALOUSY

As discussed in the earlier chapters, the partners of the association must sit down together at the earliest possible time and discuss their individual roles in the venture to arrive at an agreement as to who will perform the various tasks and how the profits will be shared. At that time, a firm arrangement is made and is then confirmed in the joint venture agreement. Problems arise from the fact that no one is a seer who can exactly forecast the future. In practice, therefore, what is predicted in the rosy days of starting the project is not always precisely carried out in reality. In fact, in most cases changed circumstances cause revised relationships. And it is from this difference, between theory and practice, that there emerges the green monster of jealousy, especially when the income of the various parties relates directly to the technical effort each contributes.

The symptoms of this malady first appear as discontent expressed by one of the parties about the contribution of one or more of his associates in pursuing their portion of the work. He feels that his firm is contributing more than its required share and that, in turn, his joint venturers are getting a "free ride." This type of feeling is really nothing new when you consider how partners in any firm sometimes react to each other's contribution of effort. However, in a joint venture the consequences can become quite serious since there is very little room to readjust. In a partnership, there are usually several projects in which the firm is involved; while the accused partner may be giving too little effort on one project, he may be performing quite satisfactorily in other projects. Furthermore, in a firm there is usually a history of successful experiences together for partners to fall back upon in such times of stress. However, in a joint venture this is not the case. There is only one job, and the parties have not been together long enough to have formed the bond of friendship which can carry them over the rough spots.

There are many ways in which this type of problem can be avoided. The first and easiest is to agree to share the profits on a basis not directly tied to the amount or intensity of the technical effort. Compensation for the work would be on the basis of a multiple of the direct labor involved. Thus, by separating equity and effort, the need for comparison becomes much less important. Remember that in many ventures the share of the profits has nothing at all to do with the effort, as in the case where the lion's share of the profit goes to the firm which brought in the project.

Another method of avoiding this type of disruptive feeling is to go to the other extreme by agreeing that the profits to be derived from the venture will be exactly determined by the amount of effort. At the end of the project the exact ratio of each firm's measured effort is calculated in man-hours or direct-labor dollars. The profits are then apportioned among the partners in accordance with the percentages computed. As is usual with all solutions of problems, other problems arise. In employing the direct-ratio method, there is no way to recognize other factors contributing to the success of the project, such as extra effort in bringing in the commission or rare expertise. Another problem which may arise is the feeling that the other firm is "loading the project" with superfluous manpower. This is more likely to occur when the work is done in one or several of the offices of the firms involved. When the project is developed in a separate joint venture office, there is less chance for question. Suspicion seems to thrive on lack of knowledge.

This matter of financial unhappiness ferments particularly when the firm which has charge of one aspect of the work causes loss to the job. Imagine that your responsibility is to carry the project through the design stage, while your partner has been designated to produce the working drawings and specifications. Through carefully controlled effort, you succeed in bringing the project through your stage of responsibility with outstanding results and a healthy profit. It is now your associate's turn to demonstrate his skills on the next phase of the project. You watch the slow development of the project and the dissipation of profit through your joint venturer's lack of proper management. This hurts, especially when you can do little about it. The question is then raised: Is it better to derive the profit directly from your own actions and to let each party be responsible for not only a part of the work, but also the resultant profit or loss which results? This fee-split method has its drawbacks, of course. Do all phases of the work have the potential for the same profit? How much does the profit of each phase of the project depend upon the successful completion of the previous phase, and what does it owe to the succeeding phase? How can a truly equitable arrangement be developed which satisfies all these requirements?

These questions have, of course, been answered in many different ways. No one solution is available to respond to the varied needs of the many different types of projects and combinations of firms which the term "joint venture" includes. The one thing that is certain, however, is that the solution to the distribution of profits must be one which can weather the storms of the project and can produce an atmosphere of mutual respect and understanding throughout the duration of the undertaking. In the case where the work will be carried out in a relay-race type of organization, such that one firm completes one phase and then hands the project to the next phase, it would seem that the best solution to the sharing of profits would be one which takes individual performance into account while not losing sight of the fact that this still is an association of firms, formed for a common goal. This method might result in each firm's taking the major share of the profit earned during its phase of the work and partaking in a minor way in the profits or losses developed by the others. This type of compromise would seem to provide the best motivation to all parties while still responding to the need for a cohesive element relating to the entire venture.

This same type of solution would apply to the venture in which firms of different expertise, such as architects and engineers, are involved. Here again, harmony might best be established if the method of compensation were one by which a major part of each party's profit was directly related to the effort involved.

Continuous, good communication can go a long way in helping to dispel jealousy. This includes not only periodic reports on the technical effort, but also the necessity of keeping all parties up-to-date and well-informed in the matters of the financial situation throughout the duration of the project. If a loss is developing, everyone should know at the earliest possible instant so that any corrective action could be taken on a timely basis, with all parties in a position to contribute their expertise toward a solution.

Combating the financial jealousy factor takes time and understanding in trying to offset it before it begins, as well as an open exchange of information and feelings during the full span of the project.

MANPOWER MISERIES

Another negative factor which must be understood and provided for is the aspect of joint venturing which affects adversely the personnel of the project. The concerns of men, especially those who are assigned to separate joint venture offices, can have a stong influence on the efficiency, and consequently the profit picture, of the project. The concerns these men have for their continued prospects of promotion and growth in their home offices can be very crucial to their performance. While these factors, their symptoms, and their solutions have been discussed in Chapter 9, the topic is repeated here for emphasis. Careful preparation must be given to building up the proper manpower team for the project. Their feelings must be a concern of the venture, and the possible negative consequences should be anticipated and dealt with. Keeping everyone happy can be a very important factor in the smooth operation of the venture.

CHAPTER TWELVE

Venturing with Others

This book has been written about the combination of several firms in the design professions. However, with the changing scene of life and the development of new methods and materials, there will often be opportunities for the architect and/or engineer to combine with those outside the design professions in a joint venture to serve the needs of a client, or even to develop work for their own account.

The virtually limitless scope of possible associations ranges from a combination with a real estate developer or a contractor in order to conceive and erect a structure to the more esoteric pursuits of a research and analysis team, which establishes criteria for others to develop. Illustrative of this latter group would be a team of experts from many fields who might join together to establish the most desirable route for a new highway through a city. Since, as well as having varied technical roles to perform, each of these combinations has different participants, it would be impossible to cover every aspect of each venture. However, there are certain common factors which affect virtually all combinations, and it will be the goal of this chapter to examine these basic criteria.

The first, most important point to consider is that a joint venture is a temporary form of partnership. As such, each party is liable for the acts of the other parties. Although this liability extends only to the work performed under the business of the venture, it is still something which must be carefully considered when associating with firms or people outside your own area of expertise or knowledge. Evaluation of alien fields becomes difficult; therefore, caution and careful consideration are urged in the selection of your nonprofessional partners.

One possibility that should also be thoroughly reviewed with accountants and attorneys is the formation of a corporation to do the work. This type of organization is possible in many states, especially where other than professional services are involved. The use of a corporation has advantages regarding liability limits and tax benefits that might be worthwhile investigating.

Many successful joint ventures have been formed and have operated to the benefit of all concerned. These combinations have usually been formed on the basis of several fundamental principles which were established at the start of the venture and were adhered to throughout the course of the undertaking. The following are some of the factors which are essential to the well-being of the successful venture.

CHOICE OF JOINT VENTURERS

Since, in many instances, the field of expertise of this diversified type of association is foreign to the design professional who wishes to joint venture, the careful selection of his partner becomes particularly critical. A schedule of the areas of expertise required for the performance of the work must be drawn up. The determination must then be made as to which of these areas may be covered through the employment of consultants and which may require the selection of a joint venturer. In the latter case, the work done by the potential associate should furnish a major part of the total effort to deserve a "piece of the action" through partnership. Other factors, of course, include the other firm's ability to help secure the job or some other significant reason which would insure selection or success.

When the only consideration is ability in technical performance, it is sometimes more difficult to evaluate who would be the best venture partner. Since state laws do not require licenses for the work of most of these nondesign professionals, there is no standard or criterion against which to measure their quality of performance.

Most helpful in the selection of these associates is the reputation they have developed in their field of practice as well as their general acceptance in society. Generally, the same procedures described in Chapter 3 of this book could be employed in the selection of nonprofessional joint venturers. Always the vital question must be: Can you live with him as your joint venture partner?

UNDERSTANDING INDIVIDUAL ROLES
AND RESPONSIBILITIES

As stressed throughout this book, the fundamental key to the success of any relationship is the defined and accepted understanding of individual roles. In the broad-scope venture, the need for the development of this understanding is most important, since the diverse nature of the combination makes it many times more difficult to define and understand. And so, as in any other venture, the first step is to list who does what. Again, this agreement must be put in writing in order to become a permanent record of understanding. Some definitions of individual tasks fall easily into place; for example, when an architect and a builder decide to offer design-build services, essentially the former designs and the latter builds. However, what happens when a team of design professionals and behavioral scientists is given the job of creating the program for a new community? Here the definition of the individual roles may become a little more confused. Despite this difficulty, a strong attempt must be made, at the earliest possible time, to discuss and define these individual roles. If nothing else, discussion helps to better understand the project, in advance of the actual execution. Further, it may serve to pinpoint the area of potential problems which may be anticipated in the project development.

With regard to responsibility, all parties are responsible for the action of all others, but each looks to his associates to be responsible for their own areas of expertise. Almost, if not all, states of the union require that a professional whose practice affects the life, health, and safety of the public submit to licensing procedures to assure the authorities that he meets the standards of professional competence demanded by the scope of his practice. And so doctors, dentists, architects, and engineers must be examined and licensed for competency. With this license comes the responsibility for practicing in a safe manner so as to avoid injury to the public. Where architects and/or engineers join together, it is fairly clear which portion of the responsibility each profession will shoulder. In fact, each, in turn, usually has professional liability insurance to cover the practice of his profession. When they join in a common venture, a separate policy is taken out to cover the entire operation. What happens, however, when a licensed professional and a nonprofessional join hands to produce a project? How are professional responsibility and liability divided? Let us take as an example the joining of a contractor and an architect in the development of a design-build package. The architect, through his license, demonstrates his responsibility for the adequacy of the design of the project, thereby providing the required protection to the public. The builder is not required to be licensed by the state. He does have, however, a general responsibility, as does everyone, to avoid at all costs acting in a negligent manner in the pursuit of his work so as to prevent injury to the public. Whose fault is it if failure occurs? Again, the response to that question lies in the words "temporary partnership," for that defines joint venture. As a result, all partners are liable for the actions of all other partners in the context of the jointly assumed project. And so, as in any joint venture, and especially one in which there are varied disciplines, it becomes extremely important to select not only the best associates available, but also ones who have each other's trust and confidence. For, once the project commences, the team members remain throughout the undertaking.

Of extreme importance is to have your attorney check the applicable state laws regarding the limitations of nonprofessionals in the practice of architecture and/or engineering. These rules may prevent the formation of this type of joint venture.

An indemnification clause in the joint venture agreement can go a long way toward protecting one firm from the failures of the others, but the best added protection is to be sure of your joint venturers' competence before joining with them. Often there is no professional liability insurance available for these mixed joint ventures. Consult a knowledgeable insurance advisor for the best protection available.

FINANCIAL ARRANGEMENTS

Here again, the diversity of possible combinations makes it impossible to generalize about interrelationships to any great degree. However, the essence of a joint venture is the sharing of all aspects of the project, and so, in line with this philosophy, the sharing of the finances would still be equally valid, despite the wide divergence of effort of the individual parties. If we follow this reasoning through to its logical conclusion, there remains no great difference in financial arrangements between the broad scope and the more homogeneous joint ventures.

Again, use the design-build venture as an example: despite the different functions of the firms involved, the division of the profits and/or losses would usually be based on the success or failure of the entire package. Correspondingly, payment must be made to each individual party for the technical effort he expended in the development of the project. Under the assumption that the architect and the builder are in a project combination, each would be compensated for his individual effort as well as receive a piece of the entire action. For example, our firm was recently involved with a real estate broker and a contractor in the development of an office building project. We were to provide the architectural/engineering services, the contractor was to construct the building, and the broker was to lease it. In this case, the agreement stipulated that we receive our normal architectural fee, the broker be paid an agreed-upon commission for leasing the space, and the contractor be entitled to his normal profit for supervising the construction of the project. An agreement was made as to the relative percentages of sharing the income from the venture. Since this project included the retention of the property for a long period of time, the projection of income as well as depreciation tax shelter for a long period of time was involved, not just the one-shot deal of the usual joint venture in which we are normally involved.

There is one important, very serious consideration to a design professional in the creation of this type of combined venture. Quite often he is asked to be involved in a speculative proposal to design, erect, and possibly own and manage a project. In order to put together this type of proposal, much early work must go into the definition of the project so that the proposal may be as realistic as possible. This means that, at the very beginning, drawings and specifications must be produced involving almost exclusively the design professional's expertise. If the project proceeds, there is usually no problem as far as payment for work accomplished is concerned. The problem is created when the project does not proceed. The architect has drawn, but the builder has not built, nor the broker leased the space. Should the architect alone bear these costs? The answer is "No." The entire venture must share in the development costs, without the major burden's falling on the architect or engineer merely because he had to make the major contribution to the early definitive stage of the work. This understanding should be agreed upon in writing before proceeding with the work.

For example, we organized a recent joint venture project to respond to a request by the government to provide an office building of 800,000 square feet in a certain location. Landowners in the particular area were asked to submit bids, in terms of yearly rental, for the erection and maintenance of the building. The joint venture partners were the landowner, the contractor, and ourselves, as architects and engineers. The object was to produce a project meeting the owner's criteria with the lowest feasible rent that would enable us to compete with the other developers in the area. In order to define the proposed rental, a building had to be drawn and specified in sufficient detail to be priced by the contractor. Most of the early work, therefore, fell on the shoulders of the architect who had to produce the drawings and outline specifications. As it happened, after the work was done and the bids submitted, the government decided that it no longer wanted office space in this particular location, and so the entire project was dropped. Most of the initial expenses had been borne by the architect in the development of the definitive drawings, which had to be submitted with the proposal. The contractor had also expended some time in determining the cost of the structure. Too often, when a project is discontinued, the design professional is left having to assume the major burden for the original costs. In this case, however, we had worked out an understanding, in advance, that there would be a sharing of the development costs on a prorated basis, whether or not the project was successful. In this way everyone shoulders equitably his portion of the development cost.

Quite often the design professional is asked by a developer to donate his expertise, at no cost to the venture, as his contribution toward his share of equity in the venture. This proposition must be carefully considered before being accepted. First, in the case described in the previous example, when the venture falls through, who loses what? The possibility of this situation's happening is in direct relationship to the speculative nature of the undertaking. Second, is the matter of this "risk factor" figured in the equity percentage that the professional has accepted? In other words, is this venture just a device for the developer to obtain inexpensive design services while hedging his risk by having someone else absorb the initial development costs?

This method of donating services, we have found, is rarely advantageous to the design professional. We have operated on the firm belief that to cover its technical effort the individual firm contributing to a venture should receive compensation above and beyond his share of the equity of the entire project. We have found that it is sometimes better to function as a hired professional without interest in a project than to contribute your entire effort in the hope for future return. It should not be construed that we are against speculative venturing with a developer. Having equity in a project has long-term financial advantages which should not be dismissed. Nor should the important expertise that your firm contributes be undervalued by assuming a financial risk disproportionate to the potential return.

Sometimes, by reason of the diverse natures of the various participants of the venture, it becomes impossible to accurately define the individual responsibilities of all the parties involved. In these instances, with the help of a knowledgeable attorney, the best definition possible should be worked out; it should include specific provisions for overall control and define methods of quickly adjudicating any controversies or misunderstandings which may arise during the operation of the venture. In all ventures, the concept of the team must be paramount. Each individual member is there to do his part, but within a clear matrix of control and responsibility. If this concept is followed, the number of problems should be minimal and controversy should be avoided.

CHAPTER THIRTEEN

Summing Up

Once the joint venture has been completed, it is time to review what type of learning experience it has been. The criterion now must be the impact on your own firm and its personnel. Taking stock at this time can help determine the future course of your firm. The self-examination of your firm covers many areas. The conclusions will vary with the particular experience as well as with the unique aspects of the individual firm.

WHAT HAS BEEN LEARNED?

The participation in the joint venture has exposed the individual firm to a new organizational structure throughout the production of the project. Are these new principles valid enough to be included in its own practice?

New Management and Administrative Techniques

Certainly there are several methods in the administration of the project which were not part of the individual's practice prior to the joining of the venture. The question remains whether the individual firm can take advantage of the experience. For example, from a joint venture partner we learned a technique of budgeting which we have used ever since. The important ingredient in this learning evaluation is the willingness and desire both to seek change and to acknowledge that some other firm's techniques may be better than your previous ones. If you are alert and sensitive, you will learn much. Perhaps one of the most important things you may learn is that the methods you have been using throughout the years are still valid. This confirmation of your firm's existing management practices is just as positive a learning experience as the discovery of a new method, technique, or practice.

New Fields of Practice

Through the joint venture you may have developed a skill in a new field or even in a new location. The venture has provided the vehicle for entry into this new area. The way that you can capitalize on this now rests with your individual firm and its ability to employ this new-found skill. Probably of all the benefits of the joint venture participation, this potential broadening of your scope of practice is one of the major advantages. The key factor is that you are now an "expert" in a new field, having developed the experience in the particular project. With this in your background, it should be easier for you to take on the next job of this type, alone or, if you still prefer, with the same or other groups.

Reaffirmation of Old Skills

This experience has provided the criterion to measure your practice against that of others. There seems to be no better measure than that of the joint venture in which firms of the same field are thrown together; here on the actual field of practice the good and the bad techniques come to light. This occasion for self-measurement covers the entire field of practice from technical aspects to such items as public relations and even methods of how to figure your overhead. Do you like what you see, or is it time to make the changes that you and your partners have so long been talking about? The alert firm will take advantage of this opportunity for evaluation.

The Big Feeling

For many firms the participation in the joint venture is the first time they have had an opportunity to participate in a large-scale project. The question then arises about how it feels to "play in the big leagues." Is this a legitimate goal for which the firm should strive? How does it feel to deal with so many other partners and people? You gain perspective about whether this is something worthwhile or, on the other hand, whether it is better to return to the smaller practice with fewer personnel, a smaller payroll, and fewer problems to worry about. Moreover, your firm's manpower, having participated in the association, come away from the experience much wiser. They have firsthand knowledge of this larger or different work. They now form your firm's reservoir of technical knowledge in these new skills. They, too, have seen how other firms function, and they spread the word to their fellow employees about the new skills they have acquired. These new ideas and methods may be as simple as a new way of detailing or dimensioning, but they now are absorbed into your firm's practice, improving the way you work.

The New Client

After employing a joint venture on a successful project, the client may be convinced to try out the combination on another project. This attitude certainly accrues to the benefit of all the joint venture members. However, there may often be occasions in which one of the members of the venture may be asked to take on a project which, by reason of its size or location, may not suit the entire joint venture. In this instance, the remainder of the venture should be informed of the client's intention to use the individual firm so that there is no reason for bad feelings.

A typical example of this type of occurrence is the joint venture of several firms which had accomplished together the design of a large building project in Washington, D.C. for the General Services Administration. This same client might have a small project in the home town of one of the joint venture partners. He would then request the particular partner to participate alone in this project. Another instance may be the venture of an architect and an engineer in a building project.

The next job may be an engineering job for which no archi-tecture is required. There is no reason why the engineer can-not take this job alone, providing there is no agreement among the partners to the contrary.

The basic principle of the joint venture is that it is a *tempo-rary* partnership that does not extend beyond the life of the particular project, unless other projects are obtained on behalf of the venture during the life of the agreement. As a result there is no legal, binding commitment among the parties to prevent them from accepting individual work from the same client after the job has been completed. The only operative factor, an individual, moral one, is to play fair with your former partners and to discuss this with them when the situa-tion arises. The fact remains, though, that each firm has been exposed to a new client who may be a source of new work for the venture as well as for the individual firms.

A Broadening Experience

Quite often in the experience of the participation in a venture, a firm is exposed in an intensive way to skills of new fields beyond the normal practice. This is especially true of the broad-scope ventures in which a very wide range of dis-ciplines may be present. After working with men of these new fields, it is legitimate to question whether you want to absorb this expertise as part of the normal practice of your own firm. In a simple example, the architect, having joint ventured with an engineer, may now want to build up his in-house staff to include engineering capabilities for which he had previously hired consultants. Since they have worked well together, it may even lead to the merger of the architecture and the engi-neering firms into one permanent organization.

A Limiting Experience

Possibly, the total positive result of the experience of partic-ipating in a joint venture may be a change in the firm's bank account and a very firm resolution to never again joint venture with others. That is the prerogative of the practitioner. How-ever, even that decision will be a more thoughtful one for the firm that has experienced the venture method of operating and then opted to never repeat it.

DEFINING THE FIRM'S FUTURE

Whether or not the venture was a success, you are now in a position to determine your future course of action. The answers to many questions regarding your future should be more evident. Do you want to joint venture again? In the same way? Or with a different type of organization, partner, project, client, or location?

Do you want to enter the new field to which you have been exposed by the joint venture project? Do you want your firm to grow to do this work alone? Do you want to change the type of organizational structure from what you now have to include different skills, or more partners or branch offices, or corporate structure? For the individual practitioner, the most basic question may be, do you want to have partners?

Do you want to change your long-range goals, or are you content to remain as you were? Maybe you never realized how well-off you really were until you had this opportunity to measure your practice.

No matter what your decision for the future, you have grown wiser, and often richer, as a result of your joint venture experience.

APPENDIX A

Operating Procedures

1. ORGANIZATION

a. Organization Chart

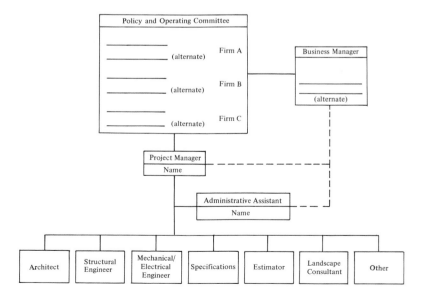

Date: _____

PROJECT NAME

PROJECT LOCATION

OPERATING PROCEDURES
FOR JOINT VENTURE OF
FIRM A

FIRM B

FIRM C
ARCHITECTS AND ENGINEERS

Policy and Operating Committee

_____ Firm A
_____ (alternate)

_____ Firm B
_____ (alternate)

_____ Firm C
_____ (alternate)

Business Manager
_____
(alternate)

Project Manager
Name

Administrative Assistant
Name

Architect | Structural Engineer | Mechanical/ Electrical Engineer | Specifications | Estimator | Landscape Consultant | Other

174

b. Operating Procedures and Responsibilities

(1) The chairman of the policy and operating committee shall transmit the decisions of the committee to whomever is concerned. In regard to the internal organization, the chain of command will flow from the chairman to the project manager, thence to the department heads or consultants. The chain of responsibility will flow in the opposite direction.

(2) The business manager shall be responsible to the policy and operating committee. He shall be responsible for the setting of budgets, review of expenditures, recommendations concerning distribution of profits, preparation and periodic distribution of financial statements, and other matters of a business and financial nature.

(3) The project manager shall be responsible to the policy and operating committee through the chairman of that committee in regard to technical matters and to the business manager in regard to business and financial matters. The project manager shall be responsible for the technical and administrative functions of the project, for compliance with the budget, for the recording of substantiating material in connection with possible extras, and for harmonious relations with the client.

2. PERSONNEL

a. The technical and administrative personnel shall normally be drawn from the home offices. When the home offices cannot supply required personnel (as mutually agreed between the home office partners and the project manager), recruitment action shall be initiated by the project manager, and the new personnel shall be put on one of the joint venture home-office payrolls. The joint venturers shall not have a payroll for this project. Each of the joint venturers shall attempt to furnish an equal number of home-office personnel to the joint venture. The project manager shall assign new men as evenly as possible to the home offices' payrolls. During the project the number of personnel assigned from the home offices shall be reviewed from time to time to determine whether equal contribution of personnel is being maintained by the home offices. The business manager may recommend corrective action, financial or otherwise.

b. The project manager will have authority over all personnel assigned to the project. He will be the final judge of the suitability of personnel assigned to the project by a home office or hired by recruitment. Personnel considered unsuitable will be returned to their home office or discharged if newly hired.

c. Requests by the project manager to the home offices for personnel shall be anticipated as far in advance of his need as possible. Conversely, return of personnel to a home office shall have as much lead time as possible.

d. Personnel assigned by a home office to this project will normally be on a permanent basis. Temporary assignments may be made when necessary. In either case, the home office and the project manager shall have an understanding as to each person's status, and this understanding shall not be abrogated by either party.

e. Hours of work, holidays, etc., will be established for the joint venture when a separate office is set up. These hours shall be adhered to by home-office personnel assigned to the joint venture except in the case of those personnel whose commuting hours are governed by train or other schedules. Such personnel shall be given some leeway in hours of work in accordance with the judgment of the project manager.

3. FINANCIAL

a. Books and records will be kept at the office of ———. All invoices from home offices will be submitted in such form and detail as determined by the joint venture accountant and paid from the joint venture account. Invoices shall normally be submitted on a monthly basis. Reimbursement to the home offices will be at such times as is determined by the business manager.

b. Accounting shall be done by ——— who shall prepare the financial statements of the joint venture. An independent auditor shall audit the books at periodic intervals.

c. The joint venture shall reimburse the home offices for the use of personnel in accordance with the following tabulation:

Title	*Location of Work*	*Charge to Joint Venture*
(1) Principals	Home office or joint venture office	$20 per hour
(2) Associates	Home office or joint venture office	$10 per hour
(3) Technical personnel	Joint venture office	Salary plus 20% on straight time; only salary on premium time

Title	Location of Work	Charge to Joint Venture
(4) Technical personnel	Home office	Salary plus 85% on straight time; only salary on premium time
(5) Clerical personnel	Home office or joint venture office	Salary plus 20% on straight time and premium time

d. The principals and associates referred to in the above paragraph are: (list all firms' principals) and (list all firms' associates).

e. Time spent on the following activities by other than full-time employees assigned to the joint venture shall *not* be charged:

   (1) Discussions or reading of technical and administrative correspondence with a view toward keeping current with project development
   (2) Attendance at policy and operating committee meetings
   (3) Considerations of home-office personnel to be assigned to the joint venture or reassigned to a home office
   (4) Any other subject which does not relate to *direct* technical or administrative effort

f. The following expenses, incurred in direct connection with this project, shall be reimbursable by the joint venture to the home offices.

   (1) Telephone (long distance)
   (2) Telegrams and cables
   (3) Travel (local, excess commutation, and long distance)
   (4) Messenger service (by outside organizations)
   (5) Specification typing (by outside organizations and by home-office personnel)
   (6) Entertainment
   (7) Mailing charges (special)
   (8) Reproductions, photos, renderings
   (9) Models
   (10) Office supplies
   (11) Recruitment expenses (advertising, agency fees)
   (12) Overtime meal allowance
   (Note: Bonuses to home-office personnel are not reimbursable by the joint venture.)

4. DISTRIBUTION OF CORRESPONDENCE AND
    INFORMATION

Until a project manager is assigned, correspondence gen-
erated by any one of the home offices shall be distributed to
each of the other home offices. Correspondence received by
one of the home offices from the client or other outside offices
shall be reproduced and distributed to the other home offices.
When a project manager is assigned, the following guide lines
shall be used:

a. Correspondence, memos, and other information shall
be considered in the following categories:
   (1) Technical
   (2) Administrative
   (3) Contractual

b. *Technical:* Dissemination of technical material shall, in
general, be confined to those personnel dealing entirely with
the technical phases of the project. The project manager will
be the focal point for reception and distribution of technical
material. His primary objective in this regard shall be to
expedite the completion of the work. Secondary objectives will
be to keep the policy board apprised of changes to the program, due dates, meetings, review comments, and other items
of significance and to keep the business manager apprised of
matters affecting the business and financial structure of the
project.

c. *Administrative:* The project manager, or an administrative
assistant acting under the project manager's direction, shall
be responsible for the material dealing with administrative
matters. In addition to those directly involved, the policy
board shall be kept informed of significant items.

d. *Contractual:* This is a special division of administrative
material which requires restrictive handling. The principle
of "need to know" will be strictly observed. The following
material will fall within this category: contract with client
(particularly portions relating to amount of fee); cash statements; income projections; calculations for extras, salaries,
and invoices; and distribution of income to home offices.
The business manager will determine the distribution and
handling of specific correspondence within this category.

APPROVED:

_____   _____   _____
Firm A   Firm B   Firm C

A Typical Joint Venture Agreement

This is a copy of a joint venture agreement which was used by an architect and an engineer, and developed prior to selection by the client. Since ventures have such variations as to venturers and undertakings, the agreement for a specific joint venture should be prepared by an attorney.

JOINT VENTURE AGREEMENT

THIS AGREEMENT made as of the   day of   between FIRM A, Architects   its principal office at   and FIRM B, INC., Engineers   having its principal office at   , and collectively hereinafter referred to as the "Joint Venturers,"

WITNESSETH:

WHEREAS, the Joint Venturers are being considered in connection with the performance of certain architectural and engineering services by (describe client and work).

WHEREAS, it is contemplated that the Joint Venturers may enter into a contract or contracts with   (Client)   for the performance of said architectural and engineering services, and may thereafter enter into further contract or contracts with   (Client)   for additional architectural and engineering services in connection therewith, relating to or resulting from the foregoing, and it is desirable for them to enter into an agreement to provide for their mutual rights and liabilities and for the performance of such services,

NOW, THEREFORE, in consideration of the premises and of the mutual promises, covenants, and agreements herein contained, the Joint Venturers agree as follows:

1. Rights of the Parties

The terms and provisions of this Agreement shall govern the relations between the parties hereto and the conduct of the work of rendering the architectural and engineering services as required under any of the aforesaid contract or contracts made or which may hereafter be made or entered into by the Joint Venturers with the   (Client)   such contract or contracts being hereinafter called the "Undertaking."

2. The Name

The name of the Joint Venture and the name under which all of its activities shall be conducted shall be   FIRM A – FIRM B ARCHITECTS AND ENGINEERS.

3. Interests of the Joint Venturers

The respective interests of the Joint Venturers in the profits and losses accruing from the Undertaking and in all property accruing from or acquired in connection with the performance of the contract or contracts constituting the Undertaking and their respective (a) obligations for contributions to working funds and disbursements, and (b) liabilities and obligations in connection with the performance of the Undertaking, shall be:

FIRM A	50%
FIRM B, INC.	50%

4. Representatives and Policy Board

As soon as may be possible after the execution of this Agreement, each Joint Venturer shall designate in writing served upon the other Joint Venturer one of its partners or associates as its principal representative and another of its partners or associates as its alternate representative to serve on a Policy Board to represent such party in the transaction of the business of the Joint Venture and in its dealings hereunder with the other Joint Venturer.

The Alternate representatives shall serve only when the principal representatives are absent or incapacitated or unable to serve. The principal and alternate representatives shall serve as such without compensation (or for such compensation, as may be agreed upon) from the funds of the Joint Venture as may be approved by the Policy Board.

Should any of the foregoing representatives die, become disabled, resign, or for any reason cease to be connected with the Joint

Venturer who nominated him, such Joint Venturer shall promptly by written notice served upon the other Joint Venturer name his successor.

Each of the Joint Venturers hereto may at any time replace either the principal or alternate representatives designated by it or all such representatives, by a notice in writing served upon the other Joint Venturer.

Meetings of the representatives of the Joint Venturers for the transaction of the business of the Joint Venture may be called at such time and such place, subject to reasonable notice, by either Joint Venturer or their representatives as they may consider necessary or desirable. None of the members of the Policy Board shall be liable to the Joint Venturers by reason of their actions as such, except in the case of their grossly negligent or actually fraudulent or dishonest conduct.

5. Supervision of the Joint Venture

The Policy Board shall have full responsibility and authority for the performance of the Undertaking, including, but not limited to, assignment of work between the Joint Venturers, preparation of schedule of work, settlement of disputes with   (Client)   , and any other matters affecting the performance of the Undertaking. Actions and decisions of the Policy Board shall be by unanimous vote and shall be final, conclusive, and binding upon the Joint Venturers.

The Policy Board shall appoint a project manager and an assistant project manager for the Undertaking, who shall (1) be responsible for the direction and management of the work in accordance with policies and procedures established by the Policy Board, (2) coordinate the work, and (3) be responsible for contacts with (Client)   and his authorized representatives.

6. Financing of Services

A joint bank account or joint bank accounts (hereinafter called the "Joint Account") shall be opened in such bank or trust company or banks or trust companies as may be determined by the Policy Board. The initial deposit in said Joint Account shall be in an amount to be determined by the Policy Board and each Joint Venturer shall contribute an amount, of which amount   FIRM A   shall contribute 50% and   FIRM B   shall contribute 50%. Each Joint Venturer shall designate an individual or individuals authorized on his behalf to endorse checks deposited in and to sign checks drawn on the said joint account or accounts.

All payments received by the Joint Venture from   (Client) or from others in connection with the Undertaking shall be promptly deposited in the Joint Account, and all invoices received by the Joint Venture shall be paid by check drawn from the said Joint Account.

The Policy Board may determine the number of signatures which may be required on any such checks drawn on such Joint

Account and may designate persons other than those who have been named by the Joint Venturers as authorized signatories to checks which may be required in the performance of the Undertaking with such limitations as to amount of such checks and number of signatures as the Policy Board may fix.

When and if the Policy Board shall determine that additional funds are required or desirable for carrying out the Undertaking or to pay any losses arising therefrom or to make good any deposits by reason of prior overpayments to the Joint Venturers, then, and in such event, the Joint Venturers shall within ten (10) days after determination by the Policy Board contribute such additional funds in the respective proportions set forth in paragraph "3" above. Should any Joint Venturer be unable or fail or neglect to contribute and deposit such additional funds in the Joint Account, then the other Joint Venturer shall have the right to advance the deficiency, and in such event, the Joint Venturer advancing such deficiency shall receive interest on such excess funds at the rate of six percent (6%) per annum from the time of their advancement to the time of their repayment. Such excess funds shall be repaid in full with interest, from the time of their advancement to the time of their repayment, from the first monies thereafter received from   (Client)   or from others in connection with the Undertaking distributable to the Joint Venturers and before any other payments are made to the Joint Venturers. The six percent (6%) interest paid for such advanced funds shall be charged against the Joint Venturer on account of whose failure the said funds were advanced.

When and if the Policy Board shall determine that the funds are in excess of the needs of the Undertaking, such excess funds shall be first applied to the return of funds advanced until such advances shall have been entirely repaid, and the balance of such excess shall be distributed to the Joint Venturers in the respective proportions set forth in paragraph "3" above. Upon final completion of the Undertaking any funds remaining after payment of all outstanding indebtednesses of the Joint Venture shall be distributed to the Joint Venturers in accordance with their respective interests as set forth in paragraph "3" above.

7. Performance of Services

The activities of the Joint Venture shall be conducted from such office or offices as the Policy Board may determine.

The Policy Board shall determine which of its activities shall be performed in any office or offices which may be maintained by the Joint Venturers.

Each of the Joint Venturers shall be reimbursed out of the funds of the Joint Venture to the extent, if any, approved by the Policy Board for costs and expenditures made or incurred by any of the Joint Venturers; the cost of doing any work on the Undertaking in the office or offices of any of the Joint Venturers and the books of account of the Joint Venture may be audited by an independent auditor selected by the Policy Board, the cost of any such audit to be paid for from the funds of the Joint Venture.

All expenses for attorneys, including the preparation of this Agreement, or for services in connection with or arising out of the Undertaking, accountants, and other professional advisers in connection with the activities of the Joint Venture, shall be charged against and paid out of the funds of the Joint Venture.

Full and current books of account for the Joint Venture shall be kept at such office as may be designated by the Policy Board, and upon such a basis (accrual or cash, calendar or fiscal) as the Policy Board may determine. For the purpose of this Agreement, the certified figures of the auditor or accountant selected by the Policy Board shall be final, conclusive, and binding upon the Joint Venturers.

8. Preliminary Expenses

All preliminary, traveling, out-of-pocket, and other expenses incurred by any Joint Venturer up to and including the date on which the contract or contracts with the   (Client)   are awarded shall be borne equally by the Joint Venturers, shall be considered a part of the cost of the Undertaking, and shall be reimbursed to the Joint Venturers out of the Joint Venture funds.

9. Technical Assistance of Each Joint Venturer

Each Joint Venturer shall make available for the Undertaking such of its personnel, facilities, experience, and records as may be reasonably necessary or desirable to the end that the Undertaking may be promptly and successfully carried out.

10. Disputes and Arbitration

Any controversy, claim, or dispute arising out of or in connection with this Agreement, or the breach thereof, or the Undertaking shall, upon the written request of either Joint Venturer, be settled by arbitration in accordance with the rules then obtaining of the American Arbitration Association, and judgment upon the award rendered upon such arbitration may be entered in the appropriate Court of any State having jurisdiction.

11. Assignment of Interest

Neither of the Joint Venturers, nor any partner of either of them, shall without the prior written consent of the other Joint Venturer sell, assign, mortgage, pledge, encumber, or in any wise dispose of any of its interest under this Agreement, or its interest in and to any monies of the Joint Venture or monies due or claimed to be due or to become due therefrom, and no such sale, assignment, mortgage, pledge, encumbrance, or other disposition shall be of any force or effect; provided, however, that any Joint Venturer may, with the prior written consent of the other Joint Venturer, assign his interest in this Joint Venture Agreement to a successor to the business of that Joint Venturer, if such succession to said business results from the voluntary action of the Joint Venturer assigning (and not from insolvency, bankruptcy or financial distress, or from an assignment for the benefit of creditors); upon such assignment the said successor shall have all the rights, duties, powers, privileges, and liabilities which the original Joint Venturer had prior to such assignment.

The right of any person, firm, or corporation claiming by, through, or under either Joint Venturer (including, but not limited to, judgment or other creditors, receivers, trustees, assignees, garnishees, executors, administrators, etc.) to assert any claim against the right, title, or interest of either Joint Venturer shall be limited in any event to the right to claim or receive after the completion of the Undertaking and after the closing of the account of the Joint Venture, the distributive share of such Joint Venturer in the net proceeds payable hereunder, whether consisting of return of any contribution made to the working funds hereunder, earnings or other avails, and then only subject to the equities of the other Joint Venturer as in this Agreement set forth.

12. Relationship of the Parties

The relationship between the Joint Venturers shall be limited to the performance of the undertaking under the terms of this Agreement, which shall be construed and be deemed to be a Joint Venture for the performance only of the Undertaking under the said contract or contracts between the Joint Venturers and   (Client)
Nothing herein contained shall be considered to constitute the Joint Venturers partners, nor to constitute either Joint Venturer the general agent of the other, nor in any manner to limit the Joint Venturers in the conduct of their respective businesses or activities, in the making of other contracts, or the performance of other work, nor to impose any liability upon either of the Joint Venturers or any of their partners except that of the performance of the terms, provisions, and conditions of this Agreement.

13. Continuity and Performance of this Agreement

One of the Joint Venturers being an individual and the other of the Joint Venturers being a corporation, to insure continued and full performance of the Joint Venture and of the Undertaking as provided in this Agreement, said individual does hereby specifically and irrevocably (until the said Undertaking is fully performed) for himself and for his executors, legal representatives, successors, and assigns, agree with the other that (a) if said individual should die or should said corporation be dissolved for whatever reason before the Undertaking is fully performed, the Joint Venture established by this Agreement shall not thereby or by reason thereof be dissolved, and (b) the executors or legal representatives of the individual Joint Venturer and successors of such corporation Joint Venturer shall respectively carry on the business of the individual or corporation for the purpose of continuing and completing the performance of the Undertaking and of this Joint Venture Agreement.

In the event either of the parties during the performance of any part of the work hereunder for any reason withdraws from the Joint

Venture or ceases to participate in the work, the other party at its discretion and subject to the consent of   (Client)   or any party with whom a contract shall be pending shall have the right to continue and complete the work. In such event, the withdrawing party shall receive no further profits or payments until completion of the entire contract and all pending work. Upon such completion, in the event there is a profit, the withdrawing party shall receive one-half the profits prorated to the degree of completion at the time of such withdrawal, and the other party shall receive all other profits. In the event there is a loss, notwithstanding when occurred, the same shall be shared equally.

14. Interpretation of this Agreement

All questions relative to the execution, validity, and interpretation of this Agreement shall be governed by the laws of the State of ——— .

15. Term of this Agreement

This Agreement shall remain in effect only for such length of time as may be necessary to carry out the Undertaking and the terms and provisions and conditions of this Agreement.

16. Persons on Whom Agreement Is Binding

The foregoing terms and provisions of this Agreement shall be binding upon and inure only to the benefit of the Joint Venturers and their respective executors, administrators, legal representatives, successors, and assigns.

17. Notices

All notice required to be given or which may be given under any of the provisions of this Agreement by either of the Joint Venturers to the other shall be given by sending such written notice to the Joint Venturer entitled thereto by mail addressed to the principal office of such Joint Venturer as first hereinabove set forth.

IN WITNESS THEREOF, the Joint Venturers hereto have hereunto affixed their hands and seals as of the day and year first above written.

WITNESS: FIRM A

                                                  By

_____   _____

ATTEST: FIRM B
                                                  A Corporation

                                                  By
                          Secretary   _____
_____
Corporate Seal

Proposed AIA Standard Form of Joint Venture Agreement

The following is the proposed text of the Agreement which has been developed by the AIA Documents Board in consultation with the author. This document appears here in draft form and may be revised before receiving the approval of the AIA Board of Directors for final official publication.

This document has been reproduced with the permission of the American Institute of Architects. Further reproduction is not authorized.

When approved and printed, the document will be available at AIA Headquarters. The user, however, should always ascertain the latest edition.

This agreement form was designed to be used when the interests of the parties are based upon a division of the profits and losses of the venture. When the *fee-split* method of division is used, modifications must be made to reflect the different methods of: payments, sharing common costs, supervision and control, financing, division of responsibilities, and other items. It is further possible that an indemnification clause, similar to the one in Chapter 7, may be desirable.

AIA DOCUMENT C801 (Proposed)

JOINT VENTURE AGREEMENT

This document has important legal consequences; consultation with an attorney is encouraged with respect to its completion or modification.

AGREEMENT

Made this   day of   in the year of Nineteen Hundred and

BETWEEN the First Party:

and the Second Party:

It is the intention of the Parties to enter into a contract or contracts with the Owner:

For the performance of professional services in connection with the Project:

And the Parties may thereafter enter into a further contract or contracts with the Owner for additional services in connection therewith, relating to or resulting from the foregoing, and it is desirable for them to enter into an agreement to provide for their mutual rights and liabilities and for the performance of such services. The Parties agree as set forth below:

I.   RIGHTS OF THE PARTIES
    a. The terms and provisions of this Agreement shall govern the relations between the parties hereto and the conduct of the work of rendering the services as required under any of the aforesaid contract or contracts made or which may hereafter be made or entered into by the Parties with the Owner, such contract or contracts being hereinafter called the "Project".
    b. This Agreement shall be governed by the Laws of the State of

II.   NAME AND PLACE OF BUSINESS
    a. The name of the Joint Venture shall be

b. The principal place of business of the Joint Venture shall be
in the State of   , or at such other
location as may be agreed upon by the Parties.

III. INTERESTS OF THE PARTIES

The respective interests of the Parties in the profits and losses
accruing from the Project and in all property accruing from or
acquired in connection with the performance of the contract or
contracts constituting the Project and their respective (a)
obligations for contributions to working funds and (b) liabilities
and obligations in connection with the performance of the
Project shall be:

   FIRST PARTY:

   SECOND PARTY:

IV. CONTRIBUTIONS

a. The initial capital contribution of each Party of the Joint
Venture shall be as follows:

   FIRST PARTY:

   SECOND PARTY:

b. Subsequent contributions shall be made in accordance with
the provisions of Article 5.

V.   REIMBURSEMENTS

a. Parties shall be reimbursed for the time of personnel used
on behalf of the Joint Venture, as set forth below:

Title	*Location*	*Charge to Joint Venture*
1. Principals	Home Office or Joint Venture Office	$ Per Hour
2. Associates	Home Office or Joint Venture Office	$ Per Hour
3. Technical Personnel	Home Office	Salary plus % on straight time; salary only on premium time
4. Technical Personnel	Joint Venture Office	Salary plus % on straight time; salary only on premium time
5. Clerical Personnel	Home Office or Joint Venture Office	Salary plus % on straight time and on premium time

b. For the purposes of this Agreement, the following are designated as Principals:

FIRST PARTY:

SECOND PARTY:

c. For the purposes of this Agreement, the following are designated as Associates:

FIRST PARTY:

SECOND PARTY:

d. Unless otherwise agreed upon the Joint Venture shall have no employees. All necessary personnel shall be provided from the staffs of the Parties. New personnel employed specifically for work on the Project will go on the payroll of one of the Parties by mutual agreement at the time of employment with distribution of new persons as agreed upon between the Parties.

e. The following expenses, incurred in direct connection with this project, shall be reimbursable at cost to the Parties, by the Joint Venture: Telephone (long distance), Telegrams and Cables, Travel (local, excess commutation, and long distance), Subsistence, Messenger Service (by outside organizations), Specification Typing (by outside organizations), Entertainment, Mailing Charges (special), Reproductions, Photographs, Renderings, Models, Office Supplies, Recruitment Expenses (ads, agency fees), Overtime Meal Allowance, and any other reimbursable item listed in the Agreement with the Owner.

VI. FISCAL YEAR

The Fiscal Year of the Joint Venture shall be

ARTICLE 1

RESPONSIBILITIES OF THE PARTIES

1.1   The Parties shall share the general obligations and responsibilities for the Project to be performed under their contract with the Owner.

1.2   Each Party shall perform the specific services required of him as set forth in the schedule attached hereto, made a part hereof, and designated as "Schedule A."

1.3 The relationship between the Parties shall be limited to the performance of the Project under the terms of this Agreement, which shall be construed and be deemed to be a Joint Venture for the performance only of the Project under the said contract or contracts between the Parties and the Owner; nor shall any liability be imposed upon either of the Parties or any of their partners except that of the performance of the terms, provisions, and conditions of this Agreement. Nothing herein contained shall be considered to constitute the Parties as partners, nor to constitute either Party the general agent of the other, nor in any manner to limit the Parties in the conduct of their respective businesses or activities, in the making of other contracts or the performance of other work.

1.4 The Parties intend that the services required of each and the responsibilities and obligations, financial and otherwise, assumed for this project shall be borne in proportion to their percentage of participation described in Paragraph III above or as may be otherwise described in this Agreement. If for any reason any Party shall be forced in any way to limit his participation in the responsibilities and obligations to less than his proportionate percentage, then his respective share of any profit or loss shall be adjusted by mutual agreement to compensate for his reduced participation.

ARTICLE 2

Representatives and Policy Board

2.1 Each Party shall designate a Principal representative to serve on a Policy Board, who shall have complete responsibility to act on behalf of that Party in any matter requiring unanimity or in any matter requiring approval from a Principal representative during the administration of the Project.

2.2 Each Party shall also designate an alternative representative to the Policy Board who shall serve only when the Principal representatives are absent or incapacitated or unable to serve. The principal and alternate representatives shall serve as such without compensation, or for such compensation from the funds of the Joint Venture as may be agreed upon by the Policy Board.

2.3 Should any of the foregoing representatives die, become disabled, resign, or for any reason cease to be connected with the Party which nominated him, such Party shall promptly by written notice served upon the other Party name his successor.

2.4 Each of the Parties hereto may at any time replace either the principal or alternate representatives designated by it or all such representatives, by a notice in writing served upon the other Party.

2.5 Meetings of the representatives of the Parties for the transaction of the business of the Joint Venture may be called at such time and such place, subject to reasonable notice, by either Party or their representatives as they may consider necessary or desirable.

ARTICLE 3

SUPERVISION OF THE JOINT VENTURE

3.1   The Policy Board shall have full responsibility and authority for the performance of the Project, including, but not limited to, assignment of work between the Parties, preparation of schedule of work, settlement of disputes with the Owner, and any other matters affecting the performance of the Project. Actions and decisions of the Policy Board shall be by unanimous vote and shall be final, conclusive, and binding upon the Parties.

3.2   The Policy Board shall appoint a project manager and an assistant project manager for the Project who shall (1) be responsible for the direction and management of the work in accordance with policies and procedures established by the Policy Board, (2) coordinate the work, and (3) be responsible for contacts with the Owner and his authorized representatives.

ARTICLE 4

ACCOUNTING

4.1   An accountant mutually agreeable to the Joint Venture shall be retained. For the purpose of this Agreement, the certified figures of the accountant shall be final, conclusive and binding upon the Parties.

4.2   One person designated by the Policy Board shall be appointed treasurer of the Joint Venture; the Treasurer shall keep for the Joint Venture a separate set of full and current books of account, and upon such a basis (accrual or cash, calendar or fiscal) as the Policy Board may determine.

4.3   The Parties shall each keep separate records based on generally accepted accounting principles detailing their participation in the Joint Venture. All such records relating to the Joint Venture shall be available to any other Party for inspection at mutually convenient times.

4.4   Records of the Joint Venture which are required to be kept subsequent to the completion of the Project pursuant to the provisions of law shall be kept at such place or places as determined by the Policy Board, and the costs thereof shall be borne by the Parties in accordance with their respective interest as described in Paragraph III.

4.5   Upon termination of the Joint Venture, all facilities and Joint Venture property shall be disposed of at the best possible price and shared in proportion to their respective interest as described in Paragraph III.

ARTICLE 5

FINANCING OF SERVICES

5.1 A joint bank account or joint bank accounts (hereinafter called the "Joint Account") shall be opened in such banks or trust companies as may be determined by the Policy Board.

5.2 Checks drawn against the Joint Account(s) shall require the signatures of two persons, each representing a different Party. Each Party shall designate an individual or individuals authorized on its behalf to endorse checks deposited in and to sign checks drawn on the said joint account or accounts.

5.3 All payments received by the Joint Venture from the Owner or from others in connection with the Project shall be promptly deposited in the Joint Account and all invoices received by the Joint Venture shall be paid by check drawn from the said Joint Account.

5.4 When and if the Policy Board shall determine that additional funds are required or desirable for carrying out the Project or to pay any losses arising therefrom or to make good any deficit by reason of prior overpayments to the Parties, then, and in such event, the Parties shall within ten (10) days after determination by the Policy Board contribute such additional funds in the respective proportions set forth in Paragraph III above. Should any Party be unable or fail or neglect to contribute and deposit such additional funds in the Joint Account, then the other Party shall have the right to advance the deficiency, and in such event, the Party advancing such deficiency shall receive interest on such funds at the rate of six per cent (6%) per annum from the time of their advancement to the time of their repayment. Such excess funds shall be repaid in full with interest (from the time of their advancement to the time of their repayment) from the first monies thereafter received from the Owner or from others in connection with the Project distributable to the Parties and before any other payments are made to the Parties. The interest paid for funds thus advanced shall be charged against the Party on account of whose failure the said funds were advanced.

5.5 When and if the Policy Board shall determine that the funds are in excess of the needs of the Project, such excess funds shall be first applied to the return of funds advanced until such advances shall have been entirely repaid, and the balance of such excess shall be distributed to the Parties in the respective proportions set forth in Paragraph III above. Upon final completion of the Project any funds remaining after payment of all outstanding indebtedness of the Joint Venture shall be distributed to the Parties in accordance with their respective interests as set forth in Paragraph III above.

5.6   In no event will advance distribution of preliminary profit reduce the obligation of the Parties to future expenses of the Joint Venture if these future expenses should exceed the gross compensation to the Joint Venture.

ARTICLE 6

PROPERTY

6.1   The capital contributions described in Paragraph IVa. above shall become Joint Venture property.

6.2   Other property obtained with funds of the Joint Venture is likewise designated as Joint Venture property.

6.3   Joint Venture property shall be so recorded in the Joint Venture accounts. Upon termination of the Project, the Joint Venture property shall be disposed of in accordance with Paragraph 4.5 of this Agreement.

6.4   Property made available for Joint Venture use shall remain the property of the contributing Party. A schedule of property made available for Joint Venture use by each Party is attached hereto and designated as "Schedule B". Upon termination of this Agreement, or at such other time as the Parties may agree upon, this property shall be returned to the contributing Party.

6.5   Property made available for Joint Venture use once contributed, shall not be withdrawn from Joint Venture use prior to termination without the consent of the Policy Board.

ARTICLE 7

PRELIMINARY EXPENSES

All preliminary, traveling, out-of-pocket and other expenses related to the Project incurred by any Party up to and including the date on which the contract or contracts with the Owner are awarded shall be borne by the Parties proportionately as set forth in Paragraph III above.

ARTICLE 8

TECHNICAL ASSISTANCE OF EACH PARTY

Each Party shall make available for the Project such of its personnel, facilities, experience, and records as may be reasonably necessary or desirable to the end that the Project may be promptly and successfully carried out.

ARTICLE 9

NOTICES

Written notice shall be deemed to have been duly served if delivered in person to the individual or member of the firm or to an officer of the corporation for whom it was intended, or if delivered at or sent by registered or certified mail to the last business address known to him who gives the notice.

ARTICLE 10

PUBLIC RELATIONS

All public statements and releases, including issuance of photographs, renderings, and the like for all media, are to be approved by the Policy Board. In private presentations of this Project not related to the Joint Venture and in any brochures or other releases of the parties hereto, the material shall be identified as follows:

(firm name) in association with (other firm name or names), or (joint venture name), a joint venture comprising (firm name) and (other firm name or names).

ARTICLE 11

INSURANCE

11.1   Each Party to this Joint Venture Agreement shall effect and maintain insurance to protect himself from claims under workmen's compensation acts; claims for damages because of bodily injury including personal injury, sickness or disease, or death of any of his employees or of any person other than his employees; and from claims for damages because of injury to or destruction of tangible property including loss of use resulting therefrom.

11.2   The Joint Venture will effect and maintain insurance to protect all Parties from claims arising out of the performance of professional services under this Agreement caused by any errors, omissions, or negligent acts for which the Joint Venture is legally liable. The Joint Venture shall maintain this insurance in force after completion of the Project until the expiration of any applicable Statutes of Limitation. In the event there is no such Statute specifically applicable to design and construction of buildings, this insurance shall be maintained in force by the Joint Venture for 12 years after the Date of Substantial Completion of the Project.

11.3   The Joint Venture shall effect and maintain adequate fidelity bond coverage on all persons who are directly connected with the handling of money of the Joint Venture.

ARTICLE 12

COMMENCEMENT AND TERMINATION

12.1   This Joint Venture will commence on the date of signing of this Agreement.

12.2   This Agreement shall remain in full force and effect until terminated by written agreement of the Parties hereto or until all of the purposes for which this Joint Venture has been undertaken have been accomplished and completed. In no event shall this Joint Venture be terminated until all rights and liabilities of this Agreement have been determined and satisfied.

ARTICLE 13

CONTINUANCE

In the event of death, dissolution, liquidation, or any other incapacity of any Party, the surviving Party or Parties shall complete the Project as called for in the agreement with the Owner. The estate, trustee, or other entity terminating the affairs of the departing Party shall share in any profit or loss in the same proportion as the work performed by the departing Party up to the time of his termination bears to the total share of work required under this Agreement. Nothing contained herein shall give such estate, trustee, or other entity terminating the affairs of the departing Party any right to participate in the administration of the affairs of the Joint Venture.

ARTICLE 14

ARBITRATION

14.1   All claims, disputes, and other matters in question arising out of, or relating to, this Agreement or the breach thereof, shall be decided by arbitration in accordance with the Construction Industry Arbitration Rules of the American Arbitration Association then obtaining unless the Parties mutually agree otherwise. This agreement to arbitrate shall be specifically enforceable under the prevailing arbitration law.

14.2   Notice of the demand for arbitration shall be filed in writing with the other Party or Parties to this Agreement and with the American Arbitration Association. The demand shall be made within a reasonable time after the claim, dispute, or other matter in question has arisen. In no event shall the arbitration be made after the date when institution of legal or equitable proceedings based on such claim, dispute, or other matter in question would be barred by the applicable statute of limitations.

14.3 The award rendered by the arbitration shall be final, and judgment may be entered upon it in accordance with applicable law in any court having jurisdiction thereof.

ARTICLE 15

LEGAL COUNSEL

The Joint Venture shall retain, for the duration of this Agreement, legal counsel to be mutually agreed upon for use in connection with any matters of concern to the Joint Venture which may require legal counsel or assistance.

ARTICLE 16

EXTENT OF AGREEMENT

This Agreement represents the entire and integrated agreement between the Parties and supersedes all prior negotiations, representations, or agreements, either written or oral. This Agreement may be amended only by written instrument signed by each and every Party to this Agreement.

ARTICLE 17

ASSIGNMENT OF INTEREST

17.1 None of the Parties shall, without the prior written consent of the other Party or Parties, sell, assign, mortgage, pledge, encumber, or in anywise dispose of any of its interest under this Agreement, or its interest in and to any monies of the Joint Venture or monies due or claimed to be due or to become due therefrom, and no such sale, assignment, mortgage, pledge, encumbrance or other disposition shall be of any force or effect; provided, however, that any Party may, with the prior written consent of the other Party or Parties, assign its interest in this Joint Venture Agreement to a successor to the business of that Party, if such succession to said business results from the voluntary action of the Party assigning (and not from insolvency, bankruptcy, or financial distress, or from an assignment for the benefit of creditors); upon such assignment the said successor shall have all the rights, duties, powers, privileges, and liabilities which the original Party had prior to such assignment.

17.2 The right of any person, firm, or corporation claiming by, through, or under any Party (including, but not limited to, judgment or other creditors, receivers, trustees, assignees, garnishees, executors, administrators, etc.) to assert any claim against the right, title, or interest of any Party shall be limited in any event to the right to claim or receive after the completion of the Project and after the closing of the account of the Joint Venture, the distributive share of such Party in the net proceeds payable hereunder, whether consisting of return of any contribution made to the working funds hereunder, earnings or other avails, and then only subject to the equities of the other Party or Parties as in this Agreement set forth.

ARTICLE 18

PERSONS ON WHOM AGREEMENT IS BINDING

The foregoing terms and provisions of this Agreement shall be binding upon and inure only to the benefit of the Parties and their respective executors, administrators, legal representatives, successors, and assigns.

SCHEDULE A

(Specific Services of the Parties are set forth in Paragraph 1.2 as being described in Schedule A. If this Schedule is not used for this or any other purpose, the phrase "this page blank" should be typed in the middle of the sheet.)

SCHEDULE B

(Schedule of Property set forth in Paragraph 6.4 above as being described in Schedule B. If this Schedule is not used for this or any other purpose, the phrase "this page blank" should be typed in the middle of the sheet.)

This Agreement executed the day and year first written above.

FIRST PARTY

SECOND PARTY

Index

Index